Lifting the Lid

What we do in church and why

Andy Johnson

Copyright © 2024 Andy Johnson

All Scripture quotations taken from the Holy Bible, New International Version Anglicised Copyright © 1979, 1984, 2011 Biblica

Used by permission of Hodder & Stoughton Ltd, an Hachette UK company

All rights reserved.

'NIV' is a registered trademark of Biblica UK trademark number 1448790.

Andrea

You make all this so much easier…

Acknowledgements

A few words of thanks to the people who helped me as I wrote this book. Paul Salter, Chris Surgenor and my wife Andrea gave advice and offered editorial help throughout. Thanks for the input and the support.

Thank you to the congregations of St Nicholas Perivale and Holy Trinity Aylesbury who sat through the sermons that helped me to crystallise this material in my mind. It was enormously helpful.

I deeply appreciate the friendship and encouragement of David Robinson and the words he wrote overleaf.

And finally, thank you to James Blandford-Baker for your kind words and 20+ years of support. You really do know more about this than I do.

Contents

1. Introduction	13
2. Sung Worship	21
3. Confession	33
4. Reading the Bible	47
5. The Sermon	59
6. Affirmation of Faith	73
7. Prayers	81
8. Sharing the Peace	93
9. Holy Communion	103
10. Prayer Ministry	113
11. Final Blessing	123
12. Liturgy - The words we use	135
13. Why Bother with Church?	145

This is a book which should have been written years ago! It explains to enquirer, new Christian and veteran alike why we do what do in Christian worship on a Sunday morning. Andy Johnson writes with winsome clarity and insight, setting everything from the Sermon to the Prayers and Affirmation of Faith in an orthodox scriptural Christian context. This book will surely reinvigorate and revitalise the worship of the people of God at a time when the loss of Christian memory in Western Christianity is especially acute.

With a chapter for each aspect of regular worship, the book would lend itself to group study. It offers basic Christian information without ever being patronising and manages to communicate things that we think 'everyone knows' when actually we don't (or can't remember). Used as the basis for a sermon series it could naturally lead to a wider discussion about how to do worship better in a way which is accessible for all. I warmly commend it.

The Revd Canon James Blandford-Baker
Vicar of Histon and Vicar of Impington,
Rural Dean of Northstowe.

This is a book for people who attend churches but perhaps don't fully understand why certain things are done. It is also an easy read for non-church people who are exploring the Christian faith and may feel that churches appear foreign and irrelevant to modern life.

Andy explains clearly and simply the activities that take place in church in a theological but easy to understand way. At the same time, he educates the Christian who is seeking to understand more. In a non-threatening way, this book explains why each component part of a church service is necessary and important.

Revelation is vital to the Christian faith and *Lifting the Lid* is an excellent title for this book because it describes in simple terms the reasons why we believe what we do and most importantly why we believe all this to be true.

The first Christians devoted themselves to the teaching of Jesus and the apostles - they were eager to learn all they could. Once a person truly comes to Christ there should be a hunger and thirst to go deeper with God and to put down deep roots in Scripture. This book encourages us all to go deeper with God and to encounter him for ourselves.

Lifting the Lid deserves to be read, discussed and used as a resource for small groups because of its sheer readability. It 'de-mystifies' what is done and why and the personal stories that Andy shares will really resonate with the reader. You will see that all the activities mentioned in the book come together to form a corporate act of worship.

Many people are rightly concerned about the future shape of the church. This is a timely, helpful book that considers why the church does what it does. Read it and enjoy it; it will help people come to Christ and encounter the living God.

I wholeheartedly recommend this book.

David Robinson LVO
Licensed Lay Minister
Formerly Personal Protection Officer
to H.M Queen Elizabeth II

One

Introduction

❀ ❀ ❀

One of the highlights of my week is a Friday afternoon visit to the gym. There I run on the treadmill, I swim (a little) and I relax in the sauna or steam room. I often turn up feeling lethargic and lacklustre but nearly always leave feeling rejuvenated and refreshed. But it hasn't always been this way.

For most of my adult life, I have been too scared to go in a gym. I feel like I've always had a good basic understanding of what goes on there and indeed that I might find it enjoyable but until a few of years ago I couldn't muster the courage needed to go through the door and have a look round for myself. Essentially I believed that gyms weren't for people like me - that because I am not at the peak of physical fitness, I would be judged, looked down upon, maybe even laughed at. Even if those reactions weren't actually taking place, my perception was that they would be and that alone would seriously impinge on my experience.

I was worried that when I got there, I wouldn't know what to do or where to go. I had too many questions that I feared no-one would answer. Then there were the exercise machines - I would never be able to work them! I would look so silly while everyone else knew what they were doing. I would only be able to cope with this for a limited time before I gave up and stopped going.

Added to this, I wasn't altogether sure I liked the sort of person I would meet at the gym. I figured they looked pristine on the outside and looked 'the part' at the gym but I questioned what was really going on inside? They entered with their energy drink wearing their 'I get my five-a-day' t-shirt but I guessed they were really just as likely to stop off on the way home for a KFC as I was (let's face it, I had earned it). Hypocrites the lot of them.

Why did I think this would be the case? Because that is exactly what did happen 20 years ago! I signed up for a one year membership and went about three times. All very depressing. And disheartening.

Why do I tell you this? My belief is that perhaps some

people think this way about church. They have a casual, maybe even growing interest in going along, but fear of the unknown gets the better of them. We all know what it feels like to be the 'newbie' - awkward. And spiritually fit people[1] are no more fun to be around than physically fit specimens. Both are likely to suck the joy out of you and make you feel bad about yourself.

Then there's the 'machinery' of church life - the books, papers, the ceremony. How does one know what page you are supposed to be on, when to stand (or sit), what goes on at the front when everyone goes forward, plus don't even get me started with the singing!

My sense, as a vicar[2] is that we have made church quite a difficult place to come along to for the spiritually hungry or curious. It is as if we have fresh drinking water to offer in a dry and barren desert but we've surrounded it with an obstacle course to negotiate before you can access it. If you are spiritually hungry (or thirsty) or are simply a

---

[1] This concept is a complete misnomer but we perhaps tend to think that regular churchgoers are not spiritually flabby or out of shape. The truth is we are very ordinary people just like you.

[2] Throughout this book, this is the term I use because that is what I am. In other church settings they may use priest, pastor, minister or even just church leader.

little curious about what goes on in church, this is the book for you. My aim is to 'lift the lid' on the various weird and wonderful practices that we Christians get up to on a Sunday morning; to 'de-mystify' them and make them, and us, more accessible to you.

As I tell you what is done in church, I will also attempt to explain why. For with understanding comes meaning and what may seem to be ritualistic nonsense can suddenly become a means by which you experience the grace and goodness of God. You will begin to appreciate that there are gifts awaiting you…

If what I have said so far doesn't describe where you are on your faith journey, please don't stop reading now. There is another group of people this book is also intended for. Whatever your church tradition, we all end up doing the same or similar things week by week. As human beings we love familiarity and change does not come easily. As individuals, families and communities we settle into patterns, habits or practices that work well for us and feel like they do us good. There is nothing wrong with this, in fact as the archetypal 'creature of habit'[3] I

---

[3] Remember I have already told you I am at the gym every Friday afternoon, almost without fail.

positively encourage it in the church I lead. But the downside of this, especially in churches, is that we can end up doing a whole series of things with little or no understanding as to why we do them. We do them …. because that's what we do! There may be benefit in the various activities but that could be multiplied if a greater understanding of why we do them and what they mean was in place.

I remember sitting in a beautiful chapel in Merville, northern France and having the role that incense can play in worship explained as it wafted around us. Previous to that, incense had never been part of my church experience but I remember that being a significant 'aha' moment in the midst of the coughing and spluttering.

How would you score if you were tested about the various practices that go on in church? Do you think you know why we do what we do? Now this is not a test and neither should reading this book be about adding to your knowledge bank so you can impress your guests at a dinner party.

In a nutshell, for me gathering together as Church is

about encounter with God. Every time we meet together, there is an opportunity for us to encounter something of our infinite God. It is a chance to experience a little more of His vastness. Understanding why we do what we do will help in that process. It will add depth and meaning to what we say and do together. Understanding brings it alive!

At the time of writing, I have been an ordained Anglican Minister for ten years. Prior to that, I led an Independent Evangelical Church for eleven years. I have also worked in a Fresh Expression Church, been a member of a Baptist Church and my family has a strong Salvation Army background. Annually, I attend a Charismatic Christian festival and I often retreat amongst monks and nuns living out a rhythm of prayer and work. I guess I am telling you this to let you know that I've been around the block a bit! I have encountered the living God in all of these places so if you, the reader, worship in a church with slightly different practices to those that I am going to outline in this book, keep reading with an open heart and mind. Maybe I can 'demystify' some of these practices for you and open up a whole new raft of possibilities for encountering God.

I recognise that we take too much for granted concerning the language we use. Where possible, I have tried to use language in this book that is easy to understand and not 'Christian-ease'. Undoubtedly I have failed in that task at times but hopefully that won't put you off in deciding to venture into your local church.

So allow me to 'lift the lid' on church. If you have been attending for longer than you care to remember, think of this book as something of a refresher. And if you learn something about our practices that you really should have known already, keep that to yourself.

And if church hasn't featured in your life thus far, may the pages that follow equip and inspire you to venture through the door of your local church and maybe even stay right through to the end.

Two
Sung Worship

❈ ❈ ❈

Music expresses that which cannot be said
and on which it is impossible to be silent.
Victor Hugo

Singing is a human activity that seems entirely natural and even part of what it means to be human. (I recognise that birds and some animals sing as well!) What could be more typically human than the image of a parent singing a child to sleep, or indeed a child happily singing away to him/herself as they play. To sing is to be human - everyone does it. The truth is that we quite possibly sang before we spoke as our earliest ancestors communicated with each other through experimentation of the voice box. Is it any surprise then that a key component of any church service is worship of God in song, most often accompanied by music?

"But I can't sing!" I hear people say all the time. And for certain, a perceived inability to sing is incredibly isolating and those who claim that they just cannot hold a tune are often both sad about this and reluctant to join in with any sort of public singing. Gareth Malone has forged a prolific career in the UK forming choirs and generally bringing the most unlikely people together to sing. He and many others like him, claim everyone can sing given the right environment and the ability to throw off one's inhibitions. Apart from the impediments of age or physical disability, the psychological blocks that render many men and women silent when others are present or listening, can, it would seem, be coaxed away.

Historical Context

As with many of our Christian practices, it would seem that Christian worship has it roots in the Jewish music tradition that existed in the Temple and the Synagogue before and during the life of Jesus. But the New Testament tells us that Christian singing was not just a continuation of the patterns of worship that took place in the synagogue. The book of Acts contains many examples of worship or singing characterised by an outpouring of joy at a new found faith.[4] Perhaps the best

---

[4] See examples in Acts 2. 1-13, 3.8, 5. 41-42.

example is found in Acts 16. 24-25 where we are told that Paul and Silas, despite being imprisoned and severely flogged, were praying and singing hymns to God.

Not only is worship called for in the Bible, but the singing of songs is seen to be part of the joyful duty of the follower of God. Throughout the Old and New Testaments, the people of God are frequently seen composing music and performing for God's glory. And so what we do in our churches in terms of singing, composing, writing and performing songs of worship forms part of a tradition that is literally thousands of years old.

Gospel: Spirit and Truth

So what differentiates the singing we do and the music we make on a Sunday morning in church from the singing we might engage in when the radio is on, in the shower or at a concert? Essentially, what we are aiming for is more than singing and music-making - it is worship. Not that the other component parts of our Sunday gathering aren't worship too. All the practices we are looking at in this book come together to form a corporate act of worship. But singing and playing instruments in praise to God is a key component of that.

The songs and music are offered *to* God and they are *for* God. He is in no need of them but it is our duty and our joy to offer them to Him.

The Westminster Shorter Catechism[5] puts it like this (forgive the antiquated language):

Q. What is the chief end of man?
A. Man's chief end is to glorify God,
and to enjoy him forever.

The point is thus: there is no higher calling, nothing beyond worshipping God in terms of ultimate fulfilment. Worship of God is our reason for being and as we worship Him, we are truly ourselves and we participate in God's life. Singing and making music is just one way of worshipping God, but as created beings it would appear to be God's chosen way of allowing our spirit to connect with His.

This is not to deny that worship has some secondary consequences and we will look at these in a minute. But as the gospel writer John says, the sort of worshippers

---

[5] The Westminster Shorter Catechism was completed in 1647 by the Westminster Assembly - a gathering of English and Scottish theologians intended to bring the Church of England into greater conformity with the Church of Scotland.

that God seeks, are those who worship 'in Spirit and in truth.'[6]

The teaching of Jesus is clear here. Don't waste your time worshipping false idols or gods. Be undivided, devoted, wholehearted, sincere in worshipping the true God.

Deep

If our worship is to be these things, then we are going to need some help which is where the Holy Spirit comes in. He helps us to worship God truthfully and with sincerity; we worship by means of the Holy Spirit - with the aid of something or someone beyond ourselves.

Singing might be the most natural instinct ever (for us) but sung worship is or should be, supernatural at its core. It is Holy Spirit inspired or generated. There are some wonderfully evocative verses in Psalm 42 that help us understand this.

1 As the deer pants for streams of water, so my soul pants for you, my God.

2 My soul thirsts for God, for the living God.

7 Deep calls to deep in the roar of your waterfalls; all your waves and breakers have swept over me.

---

[6] John 4. 23-24

The Psalmist begins by painting the picture of a thirsty deer longing or panting for a fresh stream to drink from. So, he says, my soul thirsts for the living God. What a way to describe our desired attitude to God and worship! In the intervening verses he describes his anguish, his downheartedness; the perilous state of his soul. Then in verse 7 we find the phrase that perhaps better than any other, describes a heart that is worshipping God: 'deep calls to deep'. For me, this is the very depth of one's being crying out, reaching out to God.

This is no casual assent to the words being sung; not even a jolliness or enjoyment of a catchy melody. This is heartfelt, raw emotion expressed authentically before God. This is visceral; This is real; Joy, praise, lament, confusion all poured out to God with the help of the Spirit. What is inside us coming out into the open where it can be received and at times healed by God. This is beyond singing - this is something quite different.

Ephesians 5

This type of sung worship is urged and encouraged by the Apostle Paul in the New Testament as well:

… be filled with the Spirit, speaking to one another with psalms, hymns, and songs from the Spirit. Sing and make

music from your heart to the Lord, always giving thanks
to God the Father for everything,
in the name of our Lord Jesus Christ.
EPHESIANS 5. 18b - 20

Note that Paul urges worship to be *from the heart* and also trinitarian in nature. Worship of God as Father, Son and Holy Spirit should be implicit (and at times explicit) throughout any good worship service. I hope I am conveying to you the importance of sung worship in church services and how this is backed up by the Bible, Old and New Testament.

Why?

There needs to be a better reason for music playing an important role in our services than simply that human beings like to sing! The first and most important reason to sing in church is because God is deserving of our worship. By making it a priority to be in church on a Sunday, our lives are characterised by a priority to offer praise to God. Worship is the recognition of God's incredible worth and we do that best and most wholeheartedly when we worship together in the company of other Christians.

You can worship on your own or whilst going about other Sunday business activities but for all my life I have believed that the place in which Christians gather is truly the place to be. It is there that something special can and does happen. I say that partly because one of the beautiful things about congregational singing is its unique ability to bring people together. As people raise their voices, in unison and in harmony, we remember we are all part of the body of Christ[7]. This realisation of community is a great encouragement to us as well, bringing honour to God. Verse 19 from Ephesians 5 (above) says we are to speak to *one another* with psalms, hymns, and songs from the Spirit. As well as giving praise where it is due, we encourage one another in the process. We are lifted ourselves; we are carried and blessed in a way that singing on our own cannot do.

What songs should we sing?

A debate has ensued in every generation about the type of songs that are sung in church. What we sing *is* important. Well-chosen songs with well-chosen words can:

- Reinforce the other messages coming across in the service. They are a gift in the messages they convey.

---

[7] 1 Corinthians 12.27

(Remember we tend to be much more likely to remember a line from a song than any sentence said from the front.)

- These lyrics can strengthen and encourage us through our daily trials of life. Through them we are reminded of God's presence all of the time - not just in our worship services. They help us locate the light during dark times.
- They teach us about God. We can learn a great deal through the words we sing. As we sing them earnestly, more aspects of the character of God are revealed in our hearts.

Conclusion

Singing is a simple, natural thing - part of what it means to be human. But singing and the music that accompanies it are always mediated by culture. Every generation has its peculiarities - it invents something new - maybe re-works something old. All of it is valid, all of it worthwhile. When we get too involved in the musical genre being used in sung worship we only demonstrate that we have missed the point. Whether there is an organ or a band or a choir or a drum kit is purely down to cultural context and personal preference. Sung worship is essentially about the heart…

My understanding of sung worship in church was transformed over fifteen years ago when an experienced worship leader and song writer came to visit the church I was leading. We were a mixed group from various different church backgrounds. He urged us not to try and be like 'the church down the road' or to try and replicate what was being done elsewhere. He said that worship should be *indigenous*: uniquely reflecting the make-up of any particular congregation. If this is the case, then sung worship can be authentic and a real expression of the hopes and dreams, sorrows and sadnesses of a particular group of people.

Author and pastor Andrew Wilson describes sung worship as it really should be: "We cannot be satisfied by an anaemic, Christianised, don't-worry-be-happy routine …. it must be possible to lament and celebrate, be serious and joyful at the same time."[8] Churches that know something of this draw their material from countless places that help them give expression to who they really are.

I have never forgotten my introduction to the concept of *indigenous worship*. It has remained important to me as

---

[8] Andrew Wilson, *Spirit and Sacrament,* p22

throughout my years as a church leader. The pool of songs to choose from in worship is now wider than ever and it is certainly true that certain songs just 'work' in certain churches.

Why do we sing and make music? Because we have encountered a God who has touched our cold, hard hearts and melted them by the warmth of His love. This God loves us so much that He sent His Son to die for us, to repair and restore our broken relationship with Him so that we can know Him for eternity. Now I don't know about you, but that makes my heart sing…

Three
Confession

❀ ❀ ❀

> Confession is good for the soul.
> *Old Scottish Proverb*

An often repeated criticism of the Church is that we excel at making people feel guilty. If there is any truth in this, it is an absolute travesty. The true message of Christianity is one that brings freedom and liberty but alas we haven't always been very good at conveying that. Too often we've been obsessed with sin (especially sexual sin), and that obsession has become a massive obstacle to welcoming people in to experience the love and grace of God. This overemphasis on sin is only 'half a gospel' which is actually then no gospel at all.[9]

---

[9] The literal meaning of the word 'gospel' is good news and to major on sin without a solution is not good news at all.

For this reason, any discussion of or teaching on confession needs to be carefully handled; as does the practice of confession in a church service. It is therefore my intention to explain what the confession (and absolution) part of a liturgical service involves, together with what is asked of you and (importantly) what is not. Confession done well should be both private and public and I will explain what I mean by this a little later on.

If you are reading this book as an unchurched person[10] - as someone with no or very little understanding of what goes on in a church, can I make it clear that there is no public shaming element to confession! No-one will ever invite you to stand up and reveal your darkest secrets in front of everyone else. That is not how it works - not on your first Sunday, not ever. Rather, in the Church of England, towards the beginning of a Communion Service[11], the congregation is invited to stand, sit or kneel and say together and out loud authorised words that help us (we all say them out loud together) confess our sins to God. The fact that they are authorised, means they are carefully worded, thoughtfully prayed over and

---

[10] I am thrilled that you are! This book is absolutely written for you - so thank you for your interest.

[11] I explain Holy Communion in a later chapter.

common to all peoples across the worldwide Anglican communion[12]. There are no 'landmines' to step on clumsily that will make the congregation feel unhelpfully bad or worse than they already do. The words, are in the best sense of the word, generic. They will be provided for you in a book or on a screen - no-one expects you to know them off-by-heart. An example of such words of confession is as follows:

God of mercy,
we acknowledge that we are all sinners.
We turn from the wrong
that we have thought and said and done,
and are mindful of all that we have failed to do.
For the sake of Jesus, who died for us,
forgive us all that is past,
and help us to live each day

---

[12] The words used in Anglican churches are Bible-based and have evolved over hundreds of years. The most commonly used liturgy nowadays is called Common Worship (CW) which succeeded the Alternative Service Book (ASB) in 1980. Like the ASB, CW it is an alternative to the Book of Common Prayer (BCP) of 1662, which remains officially the normative liturgy of the Church of England. CW was drafted by the Church of England's Liturgical Commission and the material was either authorised by General Synod (sometimes with amendments) or simply commended for use by the House of Bishops. Eighty-five million people in over 165 countries call themselves Anglicans. The Church of England (sometimes known as the C of E) is the Anglican Church in England.

in the light of Christ our Lord.

Amen.

Line by line

Let me break this prayer down line-by-line so that you know what it means and can say it thoughtfully and authentically for yourself.

- I particularly like that the prayer starts with God and a declaration of His character: He is merciful. This is the whole basis upon which we come to Him like this. We come respectfully (for He is holy) but also gladly because He is kind and merciful. He wants to forgive us; He does not do so begrudgingly or because He is in some sense obliged to do so. He longs for our relationship to be restored and through Jesus that is possible.
- There is something quite freeing about publicly acknowledging that we are all sinners. This is a great leveller - we all need to say these words, vicar included. The basis for this assertion is the Bible:

For all have sinned and fall short of the glory of God.

ROMANS 3. 23

- Turning away from the wrong in our lives is the essence of repentance. Turning around (and away from) is active not passive and it moves confession from merely words said in a church to lives lived outside.[13] It is what prevents saying the confession together from being just a weekly ritual, repeated time after time, with little or no meaning beyond the page from which it is read. Turning from the wrong we have done / do, is a statement of intent.

- The wrong that we turn from is all-encompassing. It includes what we have thought (let's face it, who would want those images made public in church!), and said and done. I think that is pretty comprehensive. But the prayer goes on to acknowledge those things that we ought to have done but failed to do. Just when I was thinking that I have had a pretty good week, the list is beginning to look rather long…

- Before we sink into a mire of self-pity, the prayer changes tack and the reason why forgiveness is even possible is made clear. Not because God is nice and kind - some sort of generous grandfather who can see no evil in his darling grandchildren - but because the

---

[13] As somewhat of an aside, this is the very heart of true faith or what it really means to be a Christian. Christianity should never be simply about words or even belief. That belief must translate into action and in-so-doing it proves itself to be genuine and in a sense salvific.

Son of God, Jesus Christ took the punishment upon himself for our sin, every sin ever committed; for all of humanity's sin, past, present and future.[14] Jesus died for it; we need no longer carry it.

- We ask for forgiveness for *all* that is past - not select sins or those we can remember or those we think might be especially bad. Jesus died for all sin and we can be free from it all.[15]
- This beautiful, life-giving prayer concludes with an expression of determination and a request for help to live in the light and not in the darkness in the time that is ahead of us.[16]

When taught and understood in its proper context this is an exciting, almost thrilling prayer. And that is before we even get on to the absolution!

Private and Public

Thomas Cranmer, the leader of the English reformation and former Archbishop of Canterbury, described

---

[14] 1 John 1. 9 If we confess our sins, he is faithful and just and will forgive us our sins and purify us from all unrighteousness.

[15] Sin does have consequences and those may still have to be faced but forgiveness is on offer when we repent from and confess our sin.

[16] I am particularly fond of how this is expressed in one of the other C of E authorised forms of confession: *And grant, O most merciful Father, for his sake, that we may live a disciplined, righteous and godly life.*

confession as being "Before the face of this congregation". So in what sense is it both private and public? The Anglican Church in its breadth[17], adopts a 'middle way' approach to the practice of private confession. We do not make it an obligation that people confess to a priest, but we do give people the opportunity to do so if they wish. That is, no one is to be compelled to make their confession but it is available to all, and it is up to an individual's conscience whether they do or not. In my experience, it is a like that tool in the box that isn't used very often but occasionally is absolutely the right one for the job.

The regular way to express our confession is in public - in our Communion Service. The invitation to confession that the vicar uses prior to this prayer invariably includes an exhortation to 'draw near' to God. This paints a picture of us of kneeling before God (or throwing oneself upon Him if you prefer) in a private individual scene.[18] This is based on Hebrews 10.22 -

---

[17] Embracing the Catholic and Reformed traditions and just about everything else in between.

[18] Rembrandt's famous painting 'Return of the Prodigal Son' springs to mind.

Let us draw near to God with a sincere heart and with the full assurance that faith brings, having our hearts sprinkled to cleanse us from a guilty conscience and our bodies washed with pure water.

God is not far off during the confession (or at any other time for that matter). You should imagine yourself coming quietly, humbly and reverently before His throne of grace, as if it were just Him and you. The presence of the congregation around you, in one sense, is of no consequence. When you remember that, mumbling the words half-heartedly somehow fails to be an option. This is an intimate, emotion-charged moment.

That said, this is a prayer we say *together* thus making it a private-public moment. Too often, we make faith about 'me and God' and we forget that we, the Church, are the Bride of Christ.[19] He calls us into community.

Some of the most powerful times of confession that I have experienced have come when a congregation holds a corporate sense of responsibility. The confession of the sins of the Church or a nation or a people. At times it is entirely possible and indeed appropriate for us to

---

[19] Mark 2. 19, Ephesians 5. 22-33, Revelation 21. 2, 9-10.

make confession for ourselves and on behalf of a wider group of people.

When?

This act of confession most often (although not always) comes at the beginning of the service - it is almost the first thing we do when we come together to worship. This reflects the way we are taught to approach God; it's an acknowledgment of who He is and in the light of that, who we are. As such, it actually puts us at our ease. We may enter church feeling burdened or downcast by the weight of our sin. The act of confession lifts that burden, and frees us to worship God and participate in the service without distraction.

We don't start any conversation we may have in the same way - what is appropriate is discerned (or perhaps told!) and the conversation progresses accordingly. So it is with God. We may feel within ourselves that 'having the slate wiped clean' releases us in praise and adoration.

Invitation to Confession

Earlier, I referenced the vicar saying an invitation to confession. Here is an example of such an invitation:

Let us confess our sins in penitence and faith, firmly resolved to keep God's commandments and to live in love and peace with all.

This constitutes a call for us to make our confession to God, with sincerity and also believing that what God said He would do, in that moment He will actually do! Notice the vicar uses the pronoun 'us' reiterating that we are all in this together. The vicar's need for confession is just as real as the congregation's.

How?

The Gospel of Luke records Jesus telling a story about two men who approach God in prayer and it teaches us a lot about *how* we are to confess our sins; what sort of demeanour or attitude are we to adopt -

9 To some who were confident of their own righteousness and looked down on everyone else, Jesus told this parable: 10 "Two men went up to the temple to pray, one a Pharisee and the other a tax collector. 11 The Pharisee stood by himself and prayed: 'God, I thank you that I am not like other people – robbers, evildoers, adulterers or even like this tax collector. 12 I fast twice a week and give a tenth of all I get.'

13 "But the tax collector stood at a distance. He would not even look up to heaven, but beat his breast and said, 'God, have mercy on me, a sinner.'
14 "I tell you that this man, rather than the other, went home justified before God. For all those who exalt themselves will be humbled, and those who humble themselves will be exalted."

LUKE 18. 9-14

The Pharisee's prayer is essentially "Thank you that I am not like other people, who deep down I believe are not as good as me." The tax collector takes the completely opposite approach as all he says is "God, have mercy on me, a sinner."

Once the Romans had conducted a census of a town or village, they would determine how much tax that village would have to pay. People in the town could bid for the opportunity to become a tax collector and the person who got the job would go around and collect the amount required by the Romans plus the tax collector's share. In essence, whatever they collected over and above what was required by the Romans was theirs to keep as salary. With such a system, you can quickly see why the tax collectors of the day were so despised.

Humility is the key. If there is some part of you that thinks you have earned God's forgiveness or that you are in some way deserving of His mercy, then you have totally missed the point. There is no room for pride in this exercise. Rather we should take our lead from the tax collector in the parable. He knew he was a sinner[20] and it was all he could do to pray out the words that form the basis of our confession today: 'Lord, have mercy'.

Pharisees also waste much time and energy in self-justification. In modern society, self-justification is rife and the Pharisee in you will seek to convince yourself that you need to earn your place in the world by justifying your decisions and actions. Better to start on your knees before God, acknowledging your sin and asking God in His infinite grace and mercy to forgive you.

Self Esteem

On the 'flip-side' of the pride we see in the Pharisee in Luke 18 the equally problematic lack of self esteem. As valuable and life-giving as confession is, after it is made, we need to rise up and receive the forgiveness of God made possible through Jesus Christ. Failure to do this

---

[20] We don't know the details of his particular misdemeanours. Maybe he was amassing great personal wealth at the expense of the poor and needy of the village?

equates to being stuck in your sin and inevitable guilt and sorrow. We must resist this and the perfectionism that often lies behind it. Instead, throw yourself truly on the mercy of God and discover realism about sin and freedom from the guilt that comes with it.

Approaching God with the phrase "Have mercy on us" should not be an indication of low self esteem. Rather it is a trustful approach. It recognises our frailty and vulnerability but recognises that God's mercy is greater. It is good to be aware of how far we fall short but that knowledge doesn't defeat or conquer us. Rather, regular and heartfelt confession should teach us how to rest in the acceptance of God.

Absolution

In simple terms, the absolution is the forgiveness of God that the vicar pronounces over the people, on behalf of God. Here is an example:

Almighty God who forgives all who truly repent, have mercy on you, pardon and forgive you from all your sins, confirm and strengthen you in all goodness and keep you in life eternal.

Some people have difficulty with this and say isn't it a little like the vicar forgiving you? Isn't it supposed to be God? Of course it is God forgiving you. But in this part of the service (and one or two others) the vicar 'stands in the gap' between the people and God. It is a sacred space inhabited by one on behalf of all. It is part of what we clergy are called or set apart to do. It is part of our job. To hear words of forgiveness spoken out loud helps us to receive the truth about God and our standing before Him. It is truly a life-giving moment.

Freedom

I hope this chapter has helped you to see that the 'Confession' part of a church service is not to be taken lightly or approached in a blasé fashion but neither is it to be dreaded. Confession is a gift. It is a chance to cast off the burden of sin and live free of condemnation and guilt. All this is made possible by God's extravagant and liberating love being poured out into our lives - available to the whole world.

Four
Reading the Bible

❀ ❀ ❀

> The Bible is true, inspired, authoritative, sufficient, and at the heart of the Christian life.
>
> *Andrew Wilson*

Think with me for a moment about something you quite possibly take for granted. It could be turning on a tap and hot or cold running water coming out. You turn the key in the ignition of your car and the engine roars into life. You go to the local supermarket and the shelves are full with a huge range of items. A more modern invention might come to mind like the internet. When we want to find something out, what did we do before Google?

Now imagine having no access to a Bible - no physical copy at home, no app on your smartphone, no access to any and every translation on the internet. Imagine the only time you ever heard the words of the Bible was when it was read aloud in church. I wonder, would you hang on every word? Except what if in church it was read in a language that you couldn't understand - in Latin. What would be the point?

The public reading of Scripture is something we do every single week in church and yet, like so many things, this is often taken for granted. A brief survey of history tells us we really shouldn't do that.

This isn't the place for a detailed explanation of how we have come to have the Bible we have (and read in church) today but nonetheless as I am going to urge you to 'listen well' as the Bible is read aloud, then I should at least give you a little history by way of incentive.

The trouble with explaining the origins of the Bible is that it isn't one book but actually a collection of sixty-six books written by more than forty different authors spanning a time period estimated to be in excess of 2000 years.

It splits into the 39 books of the Old Testament (OT) and a further 27 books of the New Testament (NT). The books of the Old Testament were written over many centuries by various prophets and leaders. It was these writings that Jesus referred to as 'the Scriptures'.[21] The Old Testament isn't superseded by the New; rather they serve different purposes. The Old Testament tells the story of the people of God ending approximately 400 years before the birth of Christ and they also foretell his coming. The New Testament begins with Jesus' birth, life, ministry, death, ascension and resurrection and then continues with the life of the early church as told through letters written to the new worshipping communities by their key leaders.

It is important to remember that as Christianity was birthed, the true revelation of God was not found in a book of any description but in a person, Jesus Christ. After his return to the Father, the first Christians set about sharing the good news and establishing what would become the Christian Church. And so as the first century A.D. progressed, those in close proximity to Jesus' earthly ministry began to carefully write down what they had seen and heard; the first four books of what would later become the New Testament, Matthew, Mark, Luke and John, were the result.

---

[21] We know that Jesus cited or alluded to at least 23 of the 39 OT books. As a young Jewish man growing up, Jesus had clearly immersed himself in the scriptures.

49

Along with letters written by key leaders such as Peter and Paul came others that were widely circulated across the region; some more authentic than others, which led to confusion in the early church.

It wasn't until the early 4th century that Christian Church leaders in the known world gathered to discuss and sort out major issues relating to the faith, including which of the writings in circulation should formally be included in the Canon of Scripture.[22] Key gatherings of this nature were the Council of Nicea in A.D. 325 and the First Council of Constantinople in A.D. 381. It was not so much that these leaders decided which writings should make the final cut but more that together they recognised which carried a certain authority. The criteria used was never formally written down but broadly speaking a writing could only be included in the Bible if it was -

- If referring to the period during or after the life of Christ, written by one of Jesus' disciples (called Apostles) - someone who directly witnessed

---

[22] The process by which certain documents came to be considered as Holy Scripture is called canonisation from the Greek word 'canon' meaning measuring rod (think ruler or measuring stick). When the canon of Scripture was closed at 66 books, it meant they were authoritative and the means by which all other books should be measured.

- Jesus' ministry (such as Peter) or someone who interviewed such witnesses (such as Luke).
- Consistent with other portions of the Bible known to be valid and in line with traditional Christian teachings.
- Widely used in the Church and recognised as authoritative.

By the time the first century A.D. ended, most of the church had agreed on which books should be considered Scripture. And so through the centuries, the public reading of Scripture in Christian communities helped God's people to understand who God was, who they were, and who they were called to be.

In case you hadn't noticed, the Bible we read from in church is not in its original Hebrew and Greek form! The first English language Bible manuscripts were hand-written and produced by John Wycliffe, an Oxford professor and theologian in the late 14th century. He and his followers produced dozens of English language copies which he had translated from the Latin.[23]

---

[23] Apparently, the Pope was so infuriated by his translation of the Bible into English, that 44 years after Wycliffe had died, he ordered his bones to be dug-up, crushed, and scattered in the river!

In the 1450's, Johannes Gutenberg's invention of the printing press led to Bibles and books being produced in large quantities in a short period of time. This was essential as a movement known as the Reformation[24] was sweeping across the Church re-instating the centrality of biblical teaching at the heart of the faith, most notably that salvation came through faith in Christ, not through good works or donations to the Church.

William Tyndale was the first man to print the New Testament in the English language in 1525-26. Tyndale believed that ordinary people should be able to read (or listen to) the Bible in a language they could understand. His Bible was deemed illegal, was banned and Tyndale was eventually executed. But by then vernacular Bibles (those written in local languages) were available in various parts of Europe, enabling the Reformation movement to grow. It is interesting that much of what is good about the modern day church could be put down to the invention of the printing press enabling people to own and read their own Bible.

---

[24] In 1517, German Theologian and priest, Martin Luther, declared his intolerance of the Roman Catholic Church's corruption by nailing his objections for all to see on a church door in Wittenberg. These events and those that followed would eventually lead to the Christian Church splitting in the west into the Catholic and Protestant movements.

As Christians we are deeply reliant on Scripture, trusting that through the Bible God speaks to us today. For this reason it is central to all of our worship services. And so we read it aloud, we speak it out in our liturgy[25], we sing it in our worship songs and we listen to a talk based upon it in the form of a sermon. In relation to all the other aspects of the Christian worship service, the Bible is often referred to as a *plumb line*. This is a piece of string with a weight attached to one end, used to test if something (like a wall) is vertical and exactly straight.[26]

Everything we do in our worship service should be measured against the plumb line of the Bible to make sure it is aligned, centred and true. We ask the question, 'Is what is being said or sung, aligned with the Bible?' As we do this, God blesses us, encourages us, teaches us and challenges us through all aspects of the service.

In Church

In Anglican churches, numerous passages of Scripture are read in a service. Passages from the Old Testament, the New Testament letters (known as Epistles) and a Psalm are often read and a Gospel reading (Matthew,

---

[25] See chapter 12.

[26] www.dictionary.cambridge.org

Mark, Luke or John) will normally be included. The reading of the gospel is often a moment of high drama and spiritual importance as in some churches, all present stand when a passage from one of the four gospels is read, and sit for the other passages. Sometimes you will see the Bible or book containing the gospels being carried from the lectern right into the heart of the congregation to be read by a minister or priest.[27] For Anglicans, the Lectionary is the natural starting point in determining which Bible passages will be read.[28] This is a book or listing that contains a collection of Scripture readings appointed for each given Sunday (the lectionary extends beyond Sundays into everyday reading as well). It is organised into a three-year cycle of readings, designated A, B and C with each yearly cycle beginning on Advent Sunday (which falls between 27 November and 3 December).[29]

---

[27] Thus acknowledging the special importance of the books containing the words of Jesus.

[28] From the Latin word *Lectionarium* from which we also get the word *Lectern*.

[29] Year A focuses on Matthew's Gospel, Year B on Mark's Gospel and Year C on Luke's Gospel. John's Gospel is read throughout Easter and on other special occasions.

Although there is flexibility at various times of the year, depending on the preferences of a local congregation, the Lectionary is nearly always followed in the periods around Christmas and Easter. This ensures the whole church keeps together and that we consistently tell the key accounts of Jesus' birth, death and resurrection.

After the Bible is read in church, you will often hear the refrain, *'This is the word of the Lord'*. This begs the question, in what sense is the Bible the word of the Lord or God? It is actually helpful to use the Muslim understanding of the Quran to help us with our explanation. In Islam, the Quran is viewed as the literal words of God; words which God revealed in Arabic to Mohammed. This is why Muslims learn Arabic in order to read the Quran in it's original language, and why they think the words of the Quran are so powerful, because God (Allah to them) speaks them. For them, this book is the expression of God to humanity.

For Christians the true Word of God, the true revelation of God, is found not in a book but in a person, Jesus Christ the Son of God. God is not directly incarnate in the pages of the Bible, but in the person of Jesus. The Bible is the word of God in a derived sense - it reveals the work of God in the world, in the story of God's people through the ages, and supremely in revealing the person of Jesus the Word of God. The Bible is not dictated to one man in one language, but is the record of God at work in many people over centuries, inspired, on every page, by God's Holy Spirit. As the Thirty-Nine Articles of Religion say, Holy Scripture contains all that is necessary for salvation[30].

We have the response after the Scripture reading, 'This is the Word of the Lord', to remind us that the Scriptures point to God, and primarily to God in our Lord Jesus Christ, the word made flesh[31].

I hope the historical survey in this chapter has given you something of an understanding of how we arrived at the Bible we now have and the cost that was paid by some to make it accessible to us. This is why I will often preface the Scripture reading with something like,

'Now let us pay careful attention as we hear the word of God read to us'.

---

[30] The Thirty-Nine Articles of Religion are the historically defining statements of the doctrines and practices of the Church of England and were finalised in 1571.

[31] John 1. 14

As we hear and read the Bible, we are offered hope, direction, challenge and life - words that are true, inspired, authoritative, sufficient, and at the heart of the Christian life.[32]

---

[32] Andrew Wilson, *Spirit And Sacrament*, p20

Five

The Sermon

❦ ❦ ❦

> Preaching should make such a difference to a man who is listening that he is never the same again.
> *Dr Martyn Lloyd Jones*

According to Wikipedia, in modern language the word sermon is used in secular terms, somewhat negatively or pejoratively, to describe a lengthy or tedious speech delivered with great passion, by any person, to an uninterested audience. As a preacher with 35 years experience, I find that disheartening!

So why do we bother; why do we persist with this format? What is the preacher's hope? What in turn should the congregation's hope or expectation be?

The word sermon originates from the Latin word *sermō* meaning "discourse" and in churches the sermon has always been a talk based on and around one or more passages from the Bible. This chapter is best read in conjunction with the previous one: 'Reading the Bible'.

Jesus in Luke

If you could travel back in time to any period in history, where would you go? I would go back to the hillside overlooking the Sea of Galilee where it is believed Jesus preached the Sermon on the Mount and taught the Beatitudes.[33] Jesus was the ultimate teacher and preacher and I would have loved to have heard his words and stories first hand.

In Luke chapter 4 we read that Jesus returned to Nazareth, where he had been brought up and went into the synagogue to teach.[34] From this we see that the sermon (although it wasn't called that during this period) is an ancient phenomenon. In fact, in common with many of our Christian practices, the origins lie in Judaism. Those attending the synagogue were read the Scripture from scrolls (of course they didn't have the Bible as we

---

[33] Matthew chapters 5-7. Unsurprisingly, there is now a church standing on this site at En Tabgha near Capernaum.

[34] Luke 4. 14-30

have it today) and then the Rabbi[35] would comment and teach on it. People came from near and far to hear the Scripture expounded upon. On the occasion that Luke records, Jesus expounded it more powerfully than anyone had ever done before claiming that he was the very fulfilment of the passage from Isaiah[36] that he read.

Romans 10

But we don't just preach because preaching has always happened. In Paul's letter to the Romans we find this wonderful promise:

> 'Everyone who calls on the name of the Lord
> will be saved.'[37]
> ROMANS 10.13

Look at how the passage continues:

> How, then, can they call on the one they have not believed in? And how can they believe in the one of whom they have not heard? And how can they hear without someone preaching to them?
> ROMANS 10.14

---

[35] The Jewish teacher.

[36] Isaiah 61. 1-2

[37] The reason it is in quotation marks is because Paul is quoting the Old Testament prophet Joel 2. 32.

The love of God, made manifest in the life, death and resurrection of Jesus Christ should be at the heart of all preaching. Not that the same message is preached every week; but that this forms the bedrock, the foundation, the context of everything else we preach and teach.

And preach it we must or how else will men and women, boys and girls hear the gospel and how else will they have the opportunity to respond for themselves. A Christ-centred, gospel message of hope can be a gateway through which people can enter a new-found relationship with God. Therefore, preaching a sermon is a very great responsibility.

2 Timothy 4

We have a wonderful, liberating message to share but the gospel - the good news about Jesus Christ, is not always popular or indeed what people want to hear. In the New Testament, Paul writes to his young apprentice (Timothy) using these words:

> Preach the word; be prepared in season and out of season; correct, rebuke and encourage – with great patience and careful instruction. For the time will come when people will not put up with sound doctrine.

> Instead, to suit their own desires, they will gather round them a great number of teachers to say what their itching ears want to hear. They will turn their ears away from the truth and turn aside to myths.
>
> 2 TIMOTHY 4. 2-4

At my licensing[38] as Priest-in-charge of my previous church, I chose this reading with the hope that it would act as a reminder to me of an important part of my responsibilities. How tempting it is to give the congregation what they want to hear but Paul was unequivocal that this is not what Timothy (or indeed preachers today) should ever do. CS Lewis makes a similar point:

> "A man who first tried to guess 'what the public wants,' and then preached that as Christianity because the public wants it, would be a pretty mixture of fool and knave."[39]

Preachers are not there to entertain (although a sermon can be entertaining). Our role is to train, teach and help

---

[38] Licensing - the service at which I was formally and legally made Priest-in-Charge of St Nicholas Church by the Bishop of Willesden.

[39] CS Lewis, *Letters to Malcom: Chiefly on Prayer.*

grow the hearers as followers and disciples of Christ. This happens through consistent, biblical, faithful sermons preached week by week. Which brings me onto the purpose of the sermon which I have summarised under five headings.

Purpose

1. Teach - one should never under-estimate the impact on a person's life of sitting 'under' someone else's teaching over a sustained period of time. Not only will they nourish you but they will also play a great role in shaping who you are as a follower of Christ. This is why the New Testament says in the book of James:

Not many of you should become teachers, my fellow believers, because you know that we who teach will be judged more strictly.[40]

It is not that as the gathered church we don't learn through other parts of the service, but a very great responsibility is held by the preacher, in teaching from the Bible.

---

[40] James 3. 1

2. Encourage - a sermon should always on some level, encourage the listener. Think for a moment about the current happenings in the world.[41] A good sermon can lift our hearts and our consciousness up beyond the immediate malaise onto the Almighty One who is over all things. When a preacher successfully does that - perspectives change so that everything begins to look a little differently. It is not that we deny the reality of the world outside but rather we seek to connect every day events (good and bad) with our 'every day' God.

3. Challenge - encouragement should be coupled with challenge. A good sermon will always challenge one's thinking and actions. The preacher's intent should never be to make the listener feel guilty or bad but by God's grace to help bring about change in or reassessment of a person's life, in the light of the authority of Scripture. A balance needs to be struck because sermons that do nothing but challenge will ultimately fall on deaf ears or be delivered to empty churches! Holy Spirit inspired words of challenge will result in conviction (by God) and not condemnation.

---

[41] Relevant on any day, in any month of any year.

4. Exhort - challenge is closely linked to exhortation: to strongly encourage or urge (someone) to do something. The sermon should become a springboard to action; that we might not only be hearers of the word but 'do-ers' also. A good question to ask at the end of any sermon is "What is going to change as a result of this talk today?"
5. Provoke - finally, whenever I preach I tend to have it in mind to provoke the congregation. Maybe to question a long-held belief or way of life or to give each person space to re-consider it. You may not always agree with the preacher - in fact I firmly believe you shouldn't! But God gives all of us a mind of our own and the ability to use it. Both preacher and congregation should be life-long learners.

The Preacher

No preacher is perfect. No-one has it all worked out and neatly tied down. But the congregation does have a right to expect the preacher to have worked hard in preparing their message and ultimately to be hugely prayerful in their preparation and delivery. There should also be evidence that it remains the preacher's desire to live out what they preach. Words, intention and actions should all marry together. As a respected modern-day preacher Jonathan Lamb puts it, "A preacher's inconsistent living extinguishes our respectful listening."[42]

Dependence

When the renowned 20th Century preacher Charles Spurgeon used to climb up into his pulpit[43], he would apparently always pause at the first step and say a prayer. He would confess his own inability to speak with clarity and purpose and declare his complete dependence on the Holy Spirit of God to take his prepared words and use them for God's glory. It was probably because of this humility, that his sermons were so famous, so well received and are still read around the world today.

Any good preacher needs no convincing that they must be completely dependent upon the Holy Spirit for inspiration both in preparation and delivery. It is a fusion of Holy Scripture, Holy Spirit and Holy living.

---

[42] Jonathan Lamb, *Preaching Matters*, p147

[43] Long before sound systems and microphones, sermons were often preached from a raised platform called a pulpit to help the preacher see his congregation and ensure that he could be seen and heard by everyone.

How long?

Earlier in this chapter I said how the words 'lengthy' and 'tedious' had worked their way into the modern day definition of the word 'sermon'. Which begs the question, how long should a sermon be? The answer will depend on what sort of church you find yourself in. In some Anglican churches a sermon lasting more than 8 minutes would be frowned upon. Historically this would have been because Holy Communion is normally celebrated (with its accompanying liturgy) and traditionally the service would be over in no more than one hour. In many Anglican churches today, both sermon and service length have been extended.

At the other end of the spectrum there are denominations and churches where people may feel 'short-changed' if the sermon is less than forty-five minutes! When I was in Ethiopia a few years ago I attempted to double the length of my sermons, not only to allow for translation but because of the expectation of the average church-goer.[44]

---

[44] To be fair, if I had walked two hours to get to church, which many had done, I would probably have felt 'hard done by' if the preacher only spoke for 8 minutes!

This is entirely personal, but I have settled into speaking for about twenty minutes at a time. Over the years, I have at times been far-too long-winded and lost the congregation for five or ten minutes of the talk. There have also been plenty of occasions when I have failed to study a given passage well enough and denied the congregation the insights they came to hear. Twenty minutes allows a preacher to introduce the passage(s) well, make two or three points in the main body of the talk and then summarise succinctly and memorably.

The days of listening to one person speak for a lengthy period of time are long gone. We now live in a multi-media age and there is an expectation that visuals will play a part in most presentations. When used well, these can enhance a sermon and engage the congregation more fully. Add to this the benefits of listening again to a talk via a website or podcast and we can conclude the church is changing with the times whilst still remaining faithful to the core beliefs about preaching a sermon.[45]

---

[45] The internet is a wonderful thing! I found the text of an 'old-school' preacher warning his hearers of the evils of listening to sermons on a cassette tape! Thankfully attitudes have changed considerably.

Conclusion

As part of a preaching course I attended twenty-five years ago I read a book considered by many to be the authority on preaching sermons. In it, Haddon Robinson says, "Preaching is a living process involving God, the preacher and the congregation. No definition can pretend to capture that dynamic."[46]

What I love about what he says is that he reminds us that the congregation have a responsibility in this process too. Our hearts have to be open and expectant that God will speak to us through the preacher. If we are closed, God's message will be lost. I vividly remember as a young, enthusiastic Christian sharing at a young adults group (post-service) how the sermons were speaking to me week after week. I remember how I was met with blank faces from those who felt they had heard it all before and didn't expect to hear anything new.

As a means of communication, is preaching dead? Much-loved and respected Anglican evangelical theologian J.I. Packer certainly doesn't think so.

---

[46] Haddon W. Robinson, *Expository Preaching, Principles & Practice*, p19

"The church must live by God's Word as its necessary food and steer by that Word as its guiding star. Without preaching it is not conceivable that this will be either seen or done."[47]

In the Bible we have the words of God - able to change a person's life for the good. In the Holy Spirit we have someone who graciously takes these written words and those spoken by the preacher and applies them to our lives making them relevant and refreshing. And in the preacher we hopefully have someone who has prayed and studied and created or crafted a talk to the best of their God-given ability.

May I humbly suggest you always give the preacher a chance? Show them the respect they probably deserve by listening carefully to their words. Mull them over - consider them - ponder them and pray about them. You do not necessarily have to agree with all aspects of the sermon but because of the preparation and prayer they have faithfully put in, they at least deserve this respect from the listener.

---

[47] J.I. Packer, 'Why preach?' in *Honouring the Written Word of God: Collected Shorter Writings of J.I. Packer*, p260

For with hearts that are wide-open to receive, we can truly encounter God again in this and every part of our Sunday service.

Six
Affirmation of Faith

❀ ❀ ❀

> Be sure you put your feet in the right place,
> then stand firm.
> *Abraham Lincoln*

There is an ice cream store by the beach in a town called Quiberon in Brittany, France with the biggest selection of flavours you could ever imagine - 10-15 metres of choice catering for every possible need or preference. Why do I tell you this? Well if you are beginning to explore issues of faith and what your local churches have to offer you, you will quickly discover that we do differ, one from another and there is a great deal of choice. Some of the reasons for this are historical whilst others are simply about personal preference. Allow me to offer you a single paragraph journey through the history of the

Christian Church in the United Kingdom to provide some context.[48]

We are not sure who first brought the gospel to the British Isles or indeed when that was. The likelihood is that Christianity arrived with eastern traders and converts among the Roman military ranks, 100-200 years after the death and resurrection of Jesus[49]. Fast forward to the 16th century (I know we have missed out an awful lot of history here!) and Henry VIII's fall out with the Pope plus the Reformation (see chapter 3) and the Church of England is born. Over the ensuing 500 years it has proved hard / nigh on impossible to keep worshipping Christians together - all getting along and in agreement.[50] So groups of believers consistently began to break away and form their own churches that today are known as denominations. According to the Centre for the Study of Global Christianity[51] there are currently a

---

[48] This is not a Church History book so don't get annoyed. Also, I am fully aware that the UK is not the epicentre of the world but as far as the Anglican Communion is concerned, it is of great importance.

[49] Historians date this somewhere between AD 30-36.

[50] I am afraid this is human nature - we are going to disagree.

[51] livescience.comchristian-denominations

staggering 45,000 different denominations which is, quite frankly, ludicrous.

What does this tell us apart from the fact that Christians find it no easier to get-along than people of no faith? It tells us that when looking for a Christian Church we need to be careful that what is taught and believed is in some sense orthodox[52]. Essentially, is that church around the corner, Christian?

Back to the ice cream. *Quai Des Glaces* in Quiberon didn't offend me or concern me. In fact it was wonderful to have such a choice. But all the ice cream flavours on offer shared a few common denominators (milk, cream and sugar), otherwise they could not be rightly labelled as ice cream. So it is with the Christian Church - we unite around a common set of beliefs that define us as truly Christian even though we come in many different flavours and forms.

Many Anglican Churches will state these beliefs out loud as part of their liturgical worship in what is commonly called an Affirmation of Faith. Most commonly used in

---

[52] Biblical and in line with the historical teaching of the church.

this affirmation are the Apostles' Creed and the Nicene Creed.

The Nicene Creed[53] emerged during a time of doctrinal dispute in the Church. As the Christian Church grew, so did other similar but misleading teachings - heresy to give them their proper name. Church leaders met at the Council of Nicaea (in modern day Turkey) in AD 325 to talk through and agree upon orthodox Christian teachings and record this for generations to come. A slightly modified version was produced by a subsequent council at Constantinople in AD 381.

Dating back to the same time period, the Apostles' Creed is a slightly shorter version of the Nicene Creed. Despite its name, it was not written by the apostles[54] but was clearly thought to be in line with the apostles' teaching. Both creeds are trinitarian in structure - affirming God as Father, Son and Holy Spirit.

These statements weren't just hastily written in a bid to halt emerging heresy. They came out of a long process of

---

[53] Full name 'Niceno-Constantinopolitan Creed.

[54] Those who personally encountered Jesus during his time on the earth.

praying, thinking and doing. Throughout history they have shown themselves to be tough and durable - helping the Church to deal with the problems that have arisen.

Why?

It might seem rather formulaic to say these same (or similar) words every week but they remain some of the most important words spoken at our gatherings. What we believe as Christians and church-goers is clearly very important to the gathered congregation. Knowing what that is and speaking it out loud is of great significance. We are reminding ourselves and anyone who cares to listen, 'this is what I believe in'. What is more, what I believe in is far greater than just me or the group of people I am worshipping with today. We belong to a worldwide faith that has been in existence for over 2000 years and in 2020 had 2.5 billion adherents (out of a worldwide population of about 7.8 billion people).

Christian faith is personal (and in a sense individual) but it also doesn't belong to me or us. We share it with the Church worldwide and by affirming our faith together we are connected to that worldwide Church - both modern day and historical.

Truth and Error

Earlier I spoke about how the Bible acts as a plumb line by which we can measure thinking and doctrine and identify heresy. This is also true of the Affirmation of Faith we proclaim week by week in church. Reciting a creed doesn't ensure we remain orthodox but it does help us notice if a certain line of teaching is straying in an unorthodox direction. Congregation members don't need to be told what is orthodox teaching, with the Bible and the creeds to hand they can discern that for themselves.

If you decide to visit your local church, I recommend you find out what forms the core of their teaching and belief. Some denominations may call this their *Basis of Faith*.
All Anglican Churches assent to this orthodox Christianity[55] but not all Anglican Churches look the same. There is a commonality around belief but how faith, love and devotion are expressed towards God in worship can vary from church to church. Think of it like a sliding scale from what some are happy to call 'high church to low church'.

---

[55] See *The 39 Articles* for a more detailed list but it would not be practical to recite these in a worship service.

Broad Church

High Church has its roots in the Catholic Church (before Henry VIII intervened) and is characterised by terms such as formal, structured, ceremonial, dramatic, liturgical, reflective and contemplative. (Please note, I am not using any of these words in a negative, pejorative way - indeed I have grown to love and appreciate this churchmanship). Low Church is rooted more in the Reformation. Walk into a Church of England on the low end of the scale and you will find the service containing many or most of the same elements but in a much less formal way. It is still structured but often the service could best be described as 'stripped back' containing sung worship, prayer, teaching and sometimes Holy Communion. It is the same church but a different expression of worship. Clergy are unlikely to be robed, there won't be very much liturgy and the whole service may have a slightly more relaxed feel to it.

Even as I write this, I regret having to use these generalisations as I have probably upset most people along the entire scale. Even at my own church, we are in one sense formal and structured but at the same time relaxed and easy-going.[56]

In summary, the Anglican Church is a broad church offering formality and structure on one end of the scale, freedom and spontaneity on the other and just about everything in between.

Conclusion

Uniting around a common set of beliefs is important, hence the Affirmation of Faith. How a group of Christ-followers choose to express that faith corporately is of far less importance.

For some people an ice cream isn't an ice cream unless it is vanilla flavoured with the occasional foray into the daring world of chocolate or strawberry. Others have embraced cookies and cream, bubble gum and even phish food and would never go back. "Who's got it right?" Well that's simply the wrong question whether you're talking about ice cream or church.

---

[56] The truth is that the differences between 'high' and 'low' church are far more than stylistic. But as someone thinking about going to church, that is all you need to know right now.

Seven
Prayers

❀ ❀ ❀

*An opportunity to engage in passionate
and wholehearted dialogue with the maker,
redeemer and sustainer of all things.*
Samuel Wells

The newcomer at church will not be surprised to find that the service includes prayer! Often this weekly time of prayer is called the 'intercessions' - a simple definition of which is 'to make a plea on someone's behalf' or 'the act of praying to God on behalf of others.' In this chapter we will look at who the others might be, we will discover that Jesus prays with us and we will consider the role assigned to the congregation during this prayer time. As someone who has led intercessions on many occasions, I have to say what an incredible privilege it is to carefully choose words that describe the joy, heartache and longing in our hearts as the Church of God.

Let's be honest

Praying is not easy! Some claim to have a 'hotline' to God and seem to delight in hours spent on their knees but for most of us, despite being incredibly rewarding, prayer is a discipline to learn and a journey to travel.

We can often see ourselves and our own faith journeys in the lives of the first disciples. We, and they, are quite similar. I therefore find it fascinating and just a little comforting that they once said to Jesus, 'Lord, teach us to pray'.[57] Despite being religious men by background (Jews) they struggled to pray and connect with God.

In response, Jesus gave them a structure to follow that we, the Church, call the Lord's Prayer:

Our Father in heaven,
hallowed be your name,
your kingdom come,
your will be done,
on earth as in heaven.
Give us today our daily bread.
Forgive us our sins
as we forgive those who sin against us.
Lead us not into temptation

---

[57] Luke 11.1

but deliver us from evil.
For the kingdom, the power,
and the glory are yours
now and for ever. Amen.[58]

Sometimes the intercessor will end their time of prayer with an invitation to the congregation to say together the Lord's Prayer.[59]

If you find prayer hard, don't feel bad. If the disciples needed help to pray then why wouldn't we? Keep persevering - you will reap the rewards. I suggest you use the Lord's Prayer as the basis from which you can elaborate.

The person who leads the church in prayer has a special and important task.[60] Leading people in a short time of concentration, focus and devotion is no easy task,

---

[58] There are broadly two forms of this prayer used in protestant churches in the UK today. This is Contemporary Version - the 1988 translation of the English Language Liturgical Consultation. The Traditional Version is found in the 1662 Anglican Book of Common Prayer (BCP).

[59] In the Church of England, if it is a service containing Holy Communion, this prayer is used later in the service as it is only said once.

[60] It is not usually the vicar, but can be.

especially when you remember you are *speaking to God for the people*. This is different to the sermon, the notices, the welcome, the absolution or the final blessing which could all be classified as s*peaking to the people for God*.

The intercessions will almost always involve use of the spoken word but there is always room for creativity perhaps by using pictures, music or indeed anything that helps us bring the desires of our hearts to God.[61]

Praying *with* Jesus

Paul writing to some of the early Christians in Rome, tells us that Jesus himself is seated at the right hand of God the Father in heaven and he intercedes with/for us:

> Who then is the one who condemns? No one. Christ Jesus who died—more than that, who was raised to life—is at the right hand of God and is also interceding for us.
> ROMANS 8.34

I have to confess to not fully understanding how this works! But I am confident that this tells us that prayer is not something we do alone and that in essence it is

---

[61] I have on occasion encouraged people to write down a short prayer, fold it over and place it in a bowl which is then lifted up symbolically to God at the front. This is a powerful physical enactment of what is going on during the time of intercessory prayer.

about us joining in with the conversation that is already going on between Father, Son and Holy Spirit. What a joy and a privilege that is!

What informs / What to pray?

So how do we know what to pray? I urged you in a previous chapter not to leave your worldly worries or concerns at the church door but to use them to shape your worship and encounter with God. And so during the prayers, we ought to be given the opportunity to talk to God about national and international affairs making the news. Wars, climate change, race relations and the plight of refugees are just a few examples of the sort of topics we as the Church ought to be praying about.

For this reason the intercessor ought always to check the Sunday morning news headlines before coming to church and be prepared to amend or adjust their prayers accordingly.

On that desperately sad Sunday morning in August 1997 when news broke of the death of Princess Diana, I will never forget one latecomer rushing into church asking whether we had heard the shocking news. The reality was, of course we had and what's more we had reshaped and re-structured the whole service around the tragedy so that we could feel the pain we were all feeling and yet still worship God.

The selected Bible readings of the day should also inform the prayers offered. If they do, then the messages conveyed in the sermon can be re-enforced in the prayers, thus maintaining the strong common thread throughout the service. As a vicar, I would expect the intercessor to spend some time reading and meditating upon that Sunday's Bible passages as they prepared the intercessions.

Paul urges us in particular to pray or intercede for our leaders, 'for kings and those in authority over us'.[62] Clearly this is particularly pertinent at key times in a nation's history but it is also good practice at other times. Our democratically elected leaders (locally and nationally) may not be either the ones we voted for or acting in the way we might wish. But publicly praying for them re-directs our concerns in a meaningful way. I always find that when I pray for someone, my attitude

---

[62] 1 Timothy 2. 2

towards them is changed - often it softens.[63]

Good worship services will express something of the awe, wonder and amazement of God together with the joy He brings. But the very best services will also acknowledge our frailty and folly. The person leading the intercessions does not have to accomplish all this on their own but they do have a part to play in the overall message of the service.

By the time prayers are offered, praise and adoration will already have been said and sung. Also confession and repentance will already have been made and absolution given. This is one of the points of the service when the focus is widened and we look out beyond ourselves to others and the world around us bringing widespread needs to God.

Participatory

Where possible, intercessions should be free from theological jargon and also be participatory. In addition to saying *Amen*[64] at the end, the shape of intercessions

---

[63] In Matthew 5. 44 Jesus told his hearers they should love their enemies and pray for those who persecute them.

[64] Meaning 'so be it' or 'I agree'.

used in the Church of England allows for repetition and response such as:

Lord, in your mercy
to which the congregation respond:
Hear our prayer

The addition of this and/or other couplets mean that the prayer time is less of an uninterrupted monologue (during which, humanly speaking, one or more of us may become distracted) and has more of an emphasis on dialogue with God.[65] It is important that we all get the opportunity to take part and that we can all give our assent to what has been prayed.

Shape

I shall discuss in a later chapter, the nature and benefits of liturgy; how the words we use tend to be scripted, crafted and passed down through the generations. The person leading the intercessions should also take time to prepare their words but this time of prayer allows for creativity, spontaneity and free expression. That said, the next time you are in church, listen out for a shape to the

---

[65] Good, well structured intercessions are no more than 5-6 minutes long - not long enough to lose focus. Over-elaboration reduces the impact on the congregation.

intercessions that looks something like this:

- Focused on God - Father, Son and Holy Spirit. This is who is being addressed (note: not the congregation).
- Mindful of what God has already done. Rooting the prayers in Scripture can help the intercessor achieve this.
- Direct in what it is seeking God to do. Don't beat around the bush! Ask God to answer direct prayers.[66]
- Have some notion of the desired outcome. Pray expectantly, imagine results and be open to being the answer to the prayer.

What intercessions are not?

The intercessions should not be another sermon. Most people agree that one sermon per service is quite enough for anyone! Neither are the intercessions a party political broadcast! A large church in America that I sometimes follow online, recently challenged its congregation to say if they knew which of the two main political parties their leader supported. Over decades of ministry, he had never been political from the front and as a result the church attracted supporters of both the Democrat and Republican parties. This is some

---

[66] Ask and it will be given to you; seek and you will find; knock and the door will be opened to you. Luke 11. 9

achievement in a country where political allegiance and religion are so intertwined and so often lead to division.

As I have previously indicated, we are to pray for our government and those in authority over us. Therefore the intercessor needs to do that carefully and sensitively.

In addition to not being another sermon or a party political broadcast, neither are the intercessions the same as the notices. There is the temptation to 'break news' in the prayers but the passing on of sad news such as someone's illness or death always needs to be conveyed in a pastorally sensitive manner and at the right time.

The Collect

Finally the time of intercessory prayer is not to be confused with the Collect - a separate prayer usually prayed elsewhere in the service. The Collect is so called because it *collects together* the prayers of the people. It is a set prayer said in churches across the country and indeed throughout the worldwide Anglican communion. It changes every Sunday and is then used every morning the following week in the morning prayers said in church.

Conclusion

On the wall of the toilet of a previous church I led, we had a quote by American Theologian and ethicist, Stanley Hauerwas who said that the task of the church is to be the kind of community that:

> 'tells and tells rightly the story of Jesus.'

I love the simplicity of this and I believe that in essence each and every church service ought to be a microcosm of this. Week by week, the service as a whole tells the story of God and his grace-infused interaction with the created order, through each of its component parts. The task of the person leading the prayers is to speak back to God the needs of the people in the light of this incredible story. As I said at the beginning of this chapter - what a privilege to lead God's people in prayer!

Eight
Sharing the Peace

❀ ❀ ❀

Peace begins with a smile.
Mother Teresa

If you are reading this before attending church for the first time, you need to know that there comes a point in the service when everything comes to a halt and people get up out of their seats and begin to greet one another. To be honest, it can be slightly chaotic. "What is this?' you may ask, "is this the end of the service?" Actually, it is not, we are merely sharing the peace. So what is this strange phenomenon and why do we do it?

After the intercessions and before Holy Communion, the vicar will say something like this:
The peace of the Lord be always with you
(and we reply)
And also with you.

Then the chaos ensues!

The sharing of the peace is one of those parts of the worship service that it would be easy to overlook. It is often treated simply as an opportunity to get up from your seat and greet people you haven't seen since last Sunday or maybe to introduce yourself to somebody new.

But the peace isn't actually just a short interval that gives you the chance to stretch your legs. Rather it is something which carries with it significance and meaning.

Peace remains a much sought-after quality today both on a personal level and a global scale. In the hustle and bustle of life, we strive for peace, calm and space to reflect or take stock. Around the world, we long for peace as communities are torn apart and lives are destroyed by the ravages of war and conflict. In the Jewish understanding (and in the roots of Christianity), this notion of peace is called *Shalom* (a Hebrew concept) and it carries with it the sense of wholeness, completion and rest, not merely the absence of conflict or unrest. It is a well-being or equilibrium with God and with fellow human-beings. It is quite a beautiful word.

Centuries before Christ was on the earth Isaiah prophesied that a day would come when the wolf and the lamb would lie down together; a vision of *Shalom* that could not have been articulated more poetically.[67] Along with this Old Testament prophet, perhaps we all imagine and conceptualise a more peaceful world than the one we inhabit today.

This fuller understanding of peace or *Shalom* is almost certainly the background to Jesus' words in John's gospel:

> "Peace I leave with you; my peace I give to you. Not as the world gives do I give to you. Let not your hearts be troubled, neither let them be afraid."
>
> JOHN 14. 27

It is interesting that at this moment, Jesus' disciples are about to disperse as they see him arrested, put on trial and ultimately put to death. But he promises to give them peace "not as the world gives." The *Shalom* he

---

[67] Isaiah 11.6

offers (them and us) is ultimately brought about through the cruel events of an unjust crucifixion.

No Quick Fix

Of course what many of us long for on a day-to-day basis is for everything to *feel* okay. For the inner turmoil to quieten down and happiness to prevail. But is that really what Jesus is offering? The peace he brings stretches beyond the here and now - it is richer, deeper, and it is even eternal. It is a peace that somehow passes our understanding; a peace established and rooted in himself.[68]

With this in mind, at church when the vicar pronounces the peace over us and we are invited to respond in kind, we are being reminded and we are reminding each other of the promise that Jesus made to us. When we turn to each other to shake hands or warmly embrace, we are not just catching up with friends or welcoming newcomers, we are declaring the truth and reality of the eternal peace that Christ has secured for us and we are also taking our part in working for peace in our complicated and sometimes broken relationships.

---

[68] Philippians 4.7

The words of Jesus in Matthew's gospel also help us make sense of this part of the service.

'Therefore, if you are offering your gift at the altar and there remember that your brother or sister has something against you, leave your gift there in front of the altar. First go and be reconciled to them; then come and offer your gift.

MATTHEW 5. 23-24

As we will explore in the next chapter, during Holy Communion we receive a gift from God rather than offer one to Him. As we approach the altar to receive bread and wine, God sees our hearts; he knows if we are harbouring bitterness or unforgiveness towards someone else. During the sharing of the peace we can go some way towards making that right before we come forward. There may be an opportunity for reconciliation to take place.

Ancient Tradition

Sharing peace with one another is also an ancient Christian tradition. Not only is Jesus recorded as sharing this very greeting with his disciples before and after his resurrection[69] but the Apostle Paul begins everyone of his letters to the early church in this vein.[70] It is more than likely that in the very early days of the Church, 'Grace and peace to you' was the way Christians regularly greeted one another.

Not Superficial

The sharing of the peace should really go beyond a handshake, a hug, a smile or a nod. Having made peace with God through the confession and absolution earlier in the service, the peace gives us the opportunity to make peace with each other. The reality is, being part of a church community is not easy. What is easy is giving or taking offence and falling out with other church members. It happens in every church and has done so throughout every age. But through the sharing of the peace, we can keep short accounts with each other. We can be reconciled with one another, after which we can approach the altar with a clean heart and ready hands to receive again the gift of Christ: his body and blood given in love for us.

---

[69] John 14. 27 and John 20.19

[70] Romans 1.7, 1 Corinthians 1.3, 2 Corinthians 1.2, Galatians 1.3, Ephesians 1.2, Philippians 1.2, Colossians 1.2, 1 Thessalonians 1.1, 2 Thessalonians 1.2, 1 Timothy 1.2, 2 Timothy 1.2, Titus 1.4, Philemon 3.

But having shared the peace as part of our worship, we are then called to enact that peace in our relationships going forward: to forgive and seek forgiveness; to help carry the load of those who are hurting or struggling; to go on rejoicing with those who rejoice.

If we are honest with ourselves, it is easy to conveniently forget to do this. To live in the hurt of difficult relationships rather than the freedom of forgiveness. And so the weekly sharing of the peace is a powerful reminder of who we truly are in Christ, both individually and corporately. We are reminded we have been given peace and have been made whole by Christ. As God's people we are now called to make or offer peace and help bring about wholeness in others.

The service of worship that you and I can take part in at church is far from perfect. But the sharing of the peace provides us with one glimpse (among many) of what it will be like to be a people in the presence of God for all eternity. It is a powerful declaration of heaven on earth.

Without peace - the peace won for us by Christ and which passes all understanding, there is no true communion with God to be enjoyed. But Christ has indeed made peace for us with God by the shedding of his blood on the cross. And he invites us to enter and live in his peace today.

Practicalities

You may be nervous about sharing the peace - keen to do it right. Peace to your troubled soul!

The peace has its roots in the Old Testament greeting *Shalom aleichem* — Peace be upon you. As we have already seen, these were the words with which Jesus greeted his disciples on the day of his resurrection (John 20.19). In true Mediterranean style, these words would often have been accompanied by an embrace and a kiss on the cheek. It is probably this ritual that St Paul had in mind when he told the early Christians when gathered for worship to "greet one another with a holy kiss".[71]

So it is likely that the original sign of peace exchanged in church consisted of an embrace and a "holy kiss". Whereas today whilst that might be appropriate between people well-known to each other, it would be entirely

---

[71] Romans 16.16, 1 Corinthians 16.20, 2 Corinthians 13.12, 1 Thessalonians 5.26. Peter gives similar advice in 1 Peter 5.14.

inappropriate between relative strangers and most certainly newcomers!

Temperament plays a part here as well. Some people are quiet introverts who hate the thought of greeting other people, especially strangers. Others are gregarious and out-going and love the opportunity to do just that. So sensitivity is required.

By and large, the Church of England has settled on the good old-fashioned handshake accompanied with the exchange 'Peace be with you - and also with you.' Most people can cope with that.[72]

Beware

A word of caution to all church-goers: It is entirely possible to confuse a symbolic gesture with the thing being symbolised. At this point in the service, we are invited to share just a "sign" of peace, not really to engage in the reality of it. This means if there is some sorting out to do or reconciliation to be made, it is very unlikely that this can be done in that 30 second moment. A glance or a nod that acknowledges that a proper

---

[72] We are now in an age where Coronavirus is something we live with. The pandemic has understandably changed the way we share the peace and indeed Holy Communion itself.

conversation probably needs to take place afterwards, will probably suffice at this point. There is normally plenty of time for that after the service. Similarly, the proper catch up cannot happen at this point - the vicar will soon be calling you back to order.

Nine
Holy Communion

❀ ❀ ❀

*Asking why we should celebrate the Eucharist
is like asking why we breathe.*
Tom Wright

We really should not have any time for 'dead rituals' in church - we want what we do to be life-giving, meaningful and ultimately to lead us into a fresh encounter with God. That includes Holy Communion - also known as just Communion, the Lord's Supper, Mass or the Eucharist.

Communion is a meal even though you are only invited to consume a small amount of bread (many churches use wafers) and a sip of or dip into wine. What the bread and wine (known as the elements) might look like and how they are consumed might look slightly different in other Christian denominations but essentially almost all

Christians throughout the world share Holy Communion.[73]

Roots

The roots of this meal lie, not unusually in a pre-existing Jewish ritual called Passover and it was this that Jesus and his friends were celebrating on the night before he was crucified.[74] Passover commemorates the exodus of the children of Israel from Egypt, and is the foundation story of Jewish people and found in the book of Exodus.[75]

But on this occasion, Jesus broke bread and drank wine with his disciples and as he did so he attributed new meaning to both elements that would shape our Christian worship for ever.

Why?

So why do we do it? Firstly, it was an imperative from Jesus himself:

---

[73] The Salvation Army is the best known Christian Church that does not take Communion.

[74] Luke 22. 7-22

[75] Exodus 12. 31ff

> He took bread, gave thanks and broke it, and gave it to them, saying, 'This is my body given for you; do this in remembrance of me.'
>
> LUKE 22. 19

This is also in Matthew and Mark's gospels and it is repeated for us by Paul where he also adds some further instructions.[76]

But if we respond to the question 'Why do we celebrate Holy Communion?', by saying 'because Jesus told us to', we give an incomplete and insufficient answer. It implies there are no other good reasons to do so. Allow me introduce you to the concept of an unbroken line…

Unbroken Line

On the day when you next celebrate your birthday, that will clearly not be your day of birth. Rather it will be a day that joins together that past event *and* the present moment. Two things.

But if you choose to have a get-together, as guests arrive they may well wish you 'many happy returns' meaning

---

[76] 1 Corinthians 11. 17-34

the past event and the present moment are now linked to the future as well. Three things.

- You were born on a certain day.
- You celebrate that day on an upcoming date.
- And you will do so on that day, every year, into the future.

There is an unbroken line that connects a key past event with today, and with the future. So it is with Holy Communion.

When we break bread and drink from the cup, there is an unbroken line to an upper room in Jerusalem that runs to today and will run on into the future. In Holy Communion, the past, present and future are held together.

The Past

The past event is obvious to see. It's the meal that Jesus shared and his death on the cross the next morning. 'Do this in remembrance of me,' he said. So as we eat and drink, we remember what he did - his broken body and his shed blood. We call that to mind once again and we allow ourselves to be filled again with thanksgiving for

Jesus' sacrifice and the freedom and forgiveness we know because of it. That is the past.

The Present

The element that relates to the present may be less obvious so let us consider just how Jesus is present with us in Communion.

The key phrase you will hear in this part of the service is one that all Anglican vicars use as part of the Eucharistic Prayer. Praying over the bread and wine, we say: 'May this be to us the body and blood of our Lord Jesus Christ.'

Nothing visibly or physically will have changed about the bread and wine on the altar but in faith, we believe God answers that prayer! In no sense are we saying that the elements become the actual body and blood of Jesus although our Catholic brothers and sisters see that differently.

Rather through prayer, what is ordinary becomes in some sense, extraordinary for this purpose. For us and to us. That's why we don't put cheese on the left-over wafers afterwards for lunch or drink the wine similarly. The key phrase is 'may this be to us.' As a result, what is left is disposed of reverently.

And so, in a sacred moment, as we come forward to take Holy Communion, Jesus is present in the taking of bread and wine. And if Jesus is present, then we can and will be transformed. We are nourished by his presence.

With *this* perspective, Holy Communion offers us an opportunity to lay before God all our problems, our fears, our wonderings and worries and in so doing be nourished and sustained by God.

This is what makes Communion a *then* moment but also a *here-and-now* moment. A chance to meet the living Lord Jesus now. Past, present, - but it doesn't stop there. This continuous line also stretches into the future.

The Future

God's future for us and for His world, arrived in the present in the person of Jesus Christ. In him (pre and post resurrection) we catch a glimpse of what restored and renewed humanity looks like. So as we wait in a queue to take the elements, we look forward to what is secured for us and the meal or banquet we will share with God lasting all eternity. With that perspective, this meal becomes a foretaste of the feast that is to come. A taster if you like.

And so the continuous line stretches not only from the night of the last supper to today but also on to heaven, to eternity and to the glory we can only now glimpse. Past, present and future.

In Luke chapter 24 there is an account of two disciples on the road to Emmaus, who have an encounter with the risen Jesus. They were nourished by the person and presence of Jesus as he walked with them along the road and ultimately as he broke bread with them. They knew the Lord in 'the breaking of bread': so can we. Luke 24. 35 and indeed our Anglican liturgy reminds us of this future hope: For whenever you eat this bread and drink this cup, you proclaim the Lord's death (past event) until he comes (future event).

By the way, words are important. Our carefully crafted Communion liturgy helps us to try to do justice to the earth-shattering moment of history that was the death of Jesus Christ. It also helps us to get ready in our heads and hearts in order that we come to the Communion table in the appropriate manner - not casually or without careful reflection. We need to be thoughtful and reverent in approaching Holy Communion and yet at the same time full of gratitude and joy.

Some practicalities

Here are three practical things to bear in mind concerning Holy Communion.

- In many or most churches, the people go forward from their seat to receive the bread and wine. There, you are offered bread (or a wafer) and wine. Post-pandemic, many churches will offer you the chance to dip your wafer into the wine for consumption rather than drinking from what we call the 'common cup'.
- No-one *has* to go forward, in fact if you are new to church it is best that you don't. A good understanding of the meaning and significance of this meal is vital. However, no-one is excluded but rather, everyone can come forward and receive a simple prayer of blessing instead of bread and wine. You will find there will often be others doing just that.
- Most churches offer a gluten-free bread option and a non-alcoholic wine option for those who would prefer.

Conclusion

A final thought and it concerns the word incarnation. When we talk of the incarnation we are almost always talking about Jesus Christ coming to and partaking in our messy world. The word 'incarnation' literally means 'becoming physical'.

From the incarnation one thing we learn is that God engages with matter, with bodies and things. That is what Holy Communion is about – God using physical things to change us spiritually.

True faith is embodied faith. It is true that prayer is spiritual; but we pray with our bodies as well as our minds and hearts – and if our bodies are sick or restless or a distraction, then it is hard to pray. What is more, God hears our prayers and then often uses our bodies and the bodies of others to answer those prayers, through hands and feet etc.

We use our feet to come forward for Holy Communion and then we stretch out our hands to receive God's grace afresh. That act of stretching out one's hands is itself a prayer to be changed by Jesus; to receive from him once again.

Ten
Prayer Ministry

❀ ❀ ❀

The single biggest factor to draw people to church is a felt sense of the presence of God.

John Leach

As the service draws to a close, hopefully you will feel that God has been close to you - maybe even that He has spoken to you. He may have done that through any part of the service, from the sermon to the songs, from the Bible readings to the prayers. So the question is, what do you do with that? Is that just the blessing you take with you or do you need to do something more?

At many churches there is a prayer team standing by at the end of the service ready, willing and able to pray with you for a short time before you leave. Obviously this is entirely optional (nobody is going to force you to be prayed for!) and it will also be in some sense structured and always conducted in a sensitive and safe way.[77]

In certain circles this is called 'prayer ministry' and in this chapter I will look at the theology behind it, some Bible passages that speak into it and I will highlight best practice when praying for someone or being prayed for.

The Underlying Theology

At the outset let us examine the underlying theology behind the principle of praying expectantly for other people using what has become known as prayer ministry.

Firstly, God loves us and wants to give us good gifts. In Matthew chapter 7 we read of Jesus teaching his disciples about prayer. He makes the point that if earthly fathers give good gifts to their children how much more should we expect from our heavenly Father.

> If you, then, though you are evil, know how to give good gifts to your children, how much more will your Father in heaven give good gifts to those who ask him![78]

---

[77] By allowing yourself to be prayed for you are making yourself vulnerable and so you need to know that you are not going to be made to feel uncomfortable and that the pray-er knows what they are doing.

[78] Matthew 7. 11

This tells us when we are praying for someone, asking God for something good for them, He is ready, willing and able to answer that prayer and bless the person before you. We can pray with confidence knowing that God is not reluctant to bless his children but is kind and generous in doing so.

Secondly, in the context of Jesus promising the Holy Spirit to believers, John 14. 12 says this:

> 'Very truly I tell you, whoever believes in me will do the works I have been doing, and they will do even greater things than these, because I am going to the Father.'

The disciples have seen Jesus doing remarkable things during his earthly ministry in the power of the Holy Spirit. Now with the end of that time on earth in sight, Jesus promises them that by the same Holy Spirit, they will do similar, even greater things.

Once again this should give us confidence when praying for people in church. Not only does God want to give His children good gifts but He has also given us the Holy Spirit by whom and through whom we can see the Kingdom of God come in the lives of those for whom we pray.

With these two foundation stones in place, what is stopping us from praying expectantly for our church family? This is God's work and by His grace we get to play a part in the process of healing, restoration and encouragement for the church family - simply by being willing to pray for them.

The Bible

In the New Testament book of James, the author first of all acknowledges that people of faith will encounter trouble. In other words, no one is exempt and we shouldn't pretend that we are! What we can and should do is bring that trouble and the suffering that accompanies it with us into our worship and as we do so allow God to change both us and potentially the life situations that are difficult. According to chapter 5 our response to our trouble should be to pray (and by inference, be prayed for).

> Is anyone among you in trouble? Let them pray. Is anyone happy? Let them sing songs of praise. Is anyone among you sick? Let them call the elders of the church to pray over them and anoint them with oil in the name of the Lord.[79]

---

[79] James 5. 13-14

There are a few things here that require some further explanation.

- Firstly, an elder is broadly speaking a leader or a person of responsibility within the church. Elsewhere in the New Testament we find the criteria necessary for a person to be an elder.[80]
- The oil used for anointing is not magic! This is simply another example of something physical or tangible being used to convey the goodness or grace of God.[81]
- The sick person is made well. Is it really as simple as that? Well yes and no. I have witnessed countless numbers of people experiencing physical and emotional healing through prayer ministry (both with and without the anointing of oil). But it is not an exact science. Any and all healing is of God and comes by God. He alone knows the deepest needs of those being prayed for and ultimately He is sovereign. Sometimes we never know or understand why one person is healed and another is not.

In any event, what we have here is James urging the early Christians to pray for one another when they are sick or

---

[80] 1 Timothy 3. 1-6, Titus 1. 6-9

[81] This is similar to water being used at baptism.

in any kind of trouble. And how much more encouraging is it to have someone pray for you at church when you share your need than for them to simply smile, shrug their shoulders and wish you well.

In Romans 12. 1-8 Paul also gives us some interesting insight as to why we should welcome prayer at the end of the service. Verse 2 is particularly interesting:

> Do not conform to the pattern of this world, but be transformed by the renewing of your mind. Then you will be able to test and approve what God's will is – his good, pleasing and perfect will.

How we think about God and about ourselves is a key theme of Paul's New Testament writings. We are being bombarded by all sorts of 'voices' every day through social media, advertising, friends and family etc. These voices undoubtedly impact how we think and indeed feel in subtle and sometimes, not-so-subtle ways. By coming to church and making a conscious effort to be in the presence of God, we are choosing to listen to a different voice; one that will often counter-act or contradict those that we are hearing all around us.

But hearing God and adopting what Paul calls the 'mind of Christ'[82] is not easy. The messages we constantly receive which are often in contrast with God's message of love and hope to us, are constant and insistent.

So when an element of the service has touched us it is good to have someone pray with us to 'seal' that truth deep down within or to explore it's meaning or impact for our life some more. It is the equivalent of talking something through with a friend to tease out more meaning or relevance. Often when we take time to pray like this, the Holy Spirit reveals something further, either to the person doing the praying or the one being prayed for. When this happens it is so exciting. Many times I have been prayed for in this way and the insight that emerges has made me feel incredibly loved and cared for by God.

Some people have a real gift from God to hear His voice on behalf of others. There is no need to be freaked out by this. The New Testament is clear that such words from God are always to strengthen, encourage or comfort.[83] There's nothing to fear there!

---

[82] 1 Corinthians 2. 16

[83] 1 Corinthians 14.3

Best Practice

There are some best practice principles to be adhered to in church when praying for one another which once again should give you confidence that you can come forward for prayer.

- Men pray for men and women for women.
- If the pray-er asks if they can lay a hand on you they will only gently touch your shoulder (with permission).[84]
- The pray-er should in the first instance listen well to you before they endeavour to listen to God for you. We call this person centred prayer.[85]
- The team of people offering prayer will be trained and authorised to do so. No-one is perfect but this should give you confidence that you are in safe hands.

Whereas anyone can pray and indeed you could ask the person sitting next to you to pray for you, getting out of your seat and coming forward for prayer is a hugely important part of the process. It is active rather than passive and when we choose to follow Christ not just with our minds but with our bodies too, that choice

---

[84] This is biblical. Jesus often did this (e.g. Matthew 9. 18ff and Mark 6. 5, and so did his first disciples (e.g. Acts 9.12, 28.8).

[85] See two booklets in the *Grove Renewal Series* by John Leach.

becomes powerful. It says, 'I want what you have for me God'. It means you are expectant that God will heal, restore or speak to you and you therefore don't mind stepping out of your comfort zone.

A final word. Sometimes we don't go forward for prayer or indeed get the necessary training to be on the prayer team because we don't think we are good enough or that God would want to speak to / heal / use us. Here is the liberating truth of the matter:

> God is not interested in our ability
> but our availability to him.

When we step out of our comfort zone and ask for prayer, all sorts of good things can and do happen. But the results and outcomes are down to God and God alone, not our level of faith or eloquence in praying. That is hugely relieving and encouraging when you think about it.

Eleven
Final Blessing

❊ ❊ ❊

> Christians are not only called but 'sent':
> to live lives which glorify God.
> *Mark Earey*

As the way we gather at the beginning of a worship service is important to get right, so is the way we end a service. We try to ensure that the service doesn't just 'stop' but that as a people we are ready to re-enter life outside the church doors. Many people refer to this as being 'sent out'.

Why is this important? I have spoken to some people who claim that what we do in church is of no relevance to them or to the outside world. This breaks my heart. If the hour or so spent in church is something of an isolated event, unconnected to the rest of our lives, then I would agree, it is of limited value. But if our worship truly connects with life events that have preceded our visit to church and the challenges and opportunities that lie ahead in the week to come, then what we do is entirely relevant.

And so as worshippers we are 'sent out' to live lives that glorify God - that honour him and point others towards him. Now in reality the formal close of the service normally leads to coffee and a chat but everyone leaves the building at some point! And it is when we are back home or at work or out in the community that the true meaning and value of our faith and commitment is put to the test.

Post Communion Prayer

The first element of the ending of the service comes in the form of the post-communion prayer - the prayer that we say together at the end of Holy Communion. There are a few variations of this prayer - here is one that is commonly used:

Almighty God, we thank you for feeding us
with the body and blood of your Son Jesus Christ.
Through him we offer you our souls
and bodies to be a living sacrifice.

Send us out in the power of your Spirit
to live and work to your praise and glory. Amen.

Once again, notice how this prayer links the Communion we have shared with what comes next in our lives. Having taken the bread and wine as a reminder of Jesus' one true sacrifice[86] we then offer ourselves as 'living sacrifices' going forward. This sounds a little overwhelming but in essence this is a simple prayer of dedication where we pledge or commit ourselves to do what we can to live as obedient Christ-followers in the days and weeks ahead. In order to do this we ask for the indwelling Holy Spirit's help on a day-by-day basis.

Final Blessing

Then as the service draws to a close, the vicar or service leader gives or pronounces a blessing over the congregation. In simple terms, a blessing is a solemn act that calls upon and invokes the help of God upon a person or a group of people. Essentially, the vicar is asking or praying for God's favour to be upon the people that they may be renewed in their Christian faith and strengthened in their walk with God. This blessing can take various forms.

---

[86] Hebrews 10.14

Old Testament

In the Old Testament book of Numbers we find a prayer of blessing that is now used in liturgies all over the world. John Rutter's 'The Lord bless you and keep you' has popularised these words in recent years and made them well known to non-Christians as well as believers.

> [22] The Lord said to Moses, [23] 'Tell Aaron and his sons, "This is how you are to bless the Israelites. Say to them [24] '"The Lord bless you and keep you; [25] the Lord make his face shine on you and be gracious to you; [26] the Lord turn his face towards you and give you peace.'"
> NUMBERS 6. 22-26

It is interesting that 'bless you' is used in a whole variety of ways today. It can be almost like 'thanks' when someone is kind to you and some people even say it after a person sneezes![87]

'God bless' is used in equally vague ways ranging from 'God be with you' to simply 'have a nice day'! But the Old Testament blessing such as this one from Numbers was potentially much more significant. Take for instance the

---

[87] Originally, this was probably a prayer for the person that the sneeze wasn't an indication that they had the Bubonic plague!

pronouncement of a blessing by a dying father to his offspring. In Genesis 27 we read that Isaac is an old man and is preparing for his death. He calls for his elder son Esau so that he may *give him his blessing*. But Isaac is effectively tricked into giving that blessing to his other son Jacob who enters his father's tent and masquerades as his older brother. The key thing to note is this - a word spoken out-loud puts into effect a commitment to what is said. What is more, a word spoken out-loud cannot be taken back.[88]

As with the absolution spoken by the vicar after confession, so a priestly blessing at the end of the service is for the congregation a public confirmation that God is *for* them and goes with them. These are not 'magic words' but nonetheless they are 'weighty' for we know that words carry with them immense power and impact. With a desire to hold together all that has been said and taken place in the worship service with life in the outside world, who wouldn't want to hear the vicar pray or say that God would 'keep you'; that God would 'make his face to shine upon you and be gracious to you'; that he

---

[88] See Judges 11.35 and Isaiah 55.11.

would 'turn his (metaphorical) face towards you and give you peace'?[89] Most of us would.

New Testament

It is interesting to note that just about every letter written by Paul that we have in the New Testament ends with a blessing spoken (or in his case, written) over God's people. They are beautiful words and some are used in 'non-liturgical' churches to close their act of worship.[90]

The example we find here in Paul's second letter to the Corinthians acts as a wonderful ending to any Christian gathering; in many churches it is simply known as 'The Grace'.

> May the grace of the Lord Jesus Christ, and the love of God, and the fellowship of the Holy Spirit be with you all.
> 2 CORINTHIANS 13. 14

Notice it is Trinitarian in nature: the grace of the *Lord Jesus*, the love of *God* and the fellowship of the *Holy*

---

[89] Remember that earlier we learnt that peace in its fullest sense is *Shalom* meaning wholeness, health of body, mind and spirit and even good relationships with others.

[90] The truth is that every church has a liturgy or form of words that it regularly uses - it is just that some are not formalised or written down.

Spirit be with you all. This is a notable feature of a closing blessing - the *community* of the Godhead is with us as we are in community.

Jesus' Blessing

In Luke's gospel we read that the risen Jesus blessed his disciples as he ascended to the Father.

> When he had led them out to the vicinity of Bethany,
> he lifted up his hands and blessed them.
> While he was blessing them,
> he left them and was taken up into heaven.
> LUKE 24. 50-51

Typically the vicar will either lift up their hands for the blessing and/or make the sign of the cross. I hope you are beginning to understand that worship can or indeed should be a physical activity. You don't just engage your mind or voice but you worship using your whole body too.

At my previous church of St Nicholas Perivale, we had a wonderful tradition of extending our hands up and out towards God as the final blessing is said; I don't know where or when it started. But it is a truly wonderful gesture! What it communicates to God is 'yes Lord, I am up for anything and everything you want to give me! Every blessing, every strengthening, every equipping'. And in that moment, where possible, we wait as God imparts his good gifts to us.

We lift our hands as a powerful and striking acknowledgement that we need the power and presence of God in our lives in the hours and days ahead. That we are weak without Him; that we are desperate for Him to fill us with his Spirit. That He would fill us up as we are sent out.

The other thing that some people will do as the vicar makes the sign of the cross over the congregation is to make that same sign for themselves. I wonder if you were to ask a number of worshippers up and down the country why they make the sign of the cross at the blessing (and many will also do it during the absolution too), many may not be able to give you an answer. Some might say "Because we always do!"

As you come towards the end of this book, I hope that if you have learnt anything it is that there is always a good (and I mean by that a theological or biblical) reason why we do what we do in church. Otherwise quite frankly, what is the point! In this case, crossing yourself at the final blessing or absolution is an outward physical action to take the forgiveness and blessing of Christ *to* and *for* yourself. Your body says, 'yes Lord' as well as your mind; your body prays as well as your mind. In a sacramental way, Christ touches you as you touch yourself. In a sense it is no different to taking bread and wine at Holy Communion - it is an outward expression of an inward reality.

Today you will see footballers cross themselves (sometimes multiple times) as they enter the field of play. Now none of us knows what is going on in someone's heart at that moment but crossing oneself should not simply be a superstition or 'good luck charm'. Instead it can and should be both an act of worship and a physical manifestation of the reality of the work of the gospel in one's life.

Seasonal

A final piece of housekeeping. As already stated there is a familiarity in the Anglican liturgy and this is certainly the case when it comes to the final blessing and dismissal. But in particular seasons or on special days the liturgy is tailored to reflect the theme of the day. And so although the final blessing broadly stays the same, it can or does change to draw together the themes of the service. Here is a great example from the Christmas liturgy:

May the joy of the angels,
the eagerness of the shepherds,
the perseverance of the wise men,
the obedience of Joseph and Mary,
and the peace of the Christ child,
be yours this Christmas;
and the blessing of God almighty,
the Father, the Son and the Holy Spirit,
be among you and remain with you always.
Amen.

Final Dismissal

The service concludes with a 'final dismissal', which is not as formal as it sounds. In this refrain, we return again to the theme of 'sending out' with words such as these:

Go in peace to love and serve the Lord
In the name of Christ. Amen.

With these words echoing in our minds, we go having been reminded that our lives should be characterised by mission. We acknowledge that our time together is not only worship to God (in the fullest sense), but it enlivens our Christian calling to be outward looking and share the Gospel of Jesus Christ in the world. This does not always need to be in extraordinary ways but rather should simply be by living authentic Christian lives empowered by the Holy Spirit. We strive to live holy lives, characterised by prayer and service of others - lives that make a difference in the world.

Twelve
Liturgy -
The words we use

❊ ❊ ❊

Our liturgies are especially helpful in placing our lives within God's unfolding plan for humanity.
Marcus Throup

One of the things you will hopefully have learnt from this book is that in essence, church services are comprised of the same elements each week. I say this to encourage you because for the relative newcomer this means you can quickly begin to understand what is going on and more importantly, how you can participate. The Church over the years has chosen special words and phrases to give structure to its services and to help convey the mystery of the gospel. We call these words *liturgy*. These words are not perfect or complete but they are an attempt to do justice to the incredible truth that God's own Son came to the earth as a gift to humankind.

Across the breadth of the Christian Church, categories are applied to distinguish one tradition from another. And so for instance, some churches are classified as liturgical, and others are not. You need to know that this is somewhat misleading because regardless of tradition, some things get said every week. The difference probably lies in the fact that in 'liturgical' settings, those words are read from a book or a screen and both the leader and congregation take part. Critics of liturgical worship say it is full of arcane language and empty repetition but I would challenge this on both counts. Repeating words can lead to over-familiarity but it can also be a means by which the truth about God goes down deep inside - journeying from head to heart. As for the language, I find the authorised forms used in the Church of England to be rich, life-giving and flexible. The liturgy changes as the year goes on and as a result it helps us perfectly tell the story of God and his interaction with the world.[91]

---

[91] The flexibility is found in Common Worship, which runs to several volumes and together with the Book of Common Prayer is the official liturgical resource of the Church of England.

Structure

The chapter headings of this book may have brought no real surprises. When you go to church, most people expect to pray, listen to the Bible and hear a sermon (you might call it a talk), sing songs and be offered bread and wine. But what you might not know is an added sense that one element naturally flows from another, meaning the whole thing is not just thrown together. There is shape and purpose in the service partly because we ensure that each component is as spiritual and biblical as possible. Liturgical churches rely on their spiritual predecessors in the church to provide depth and consistency in the words they use. As a vicar, this is a great help and reassurance to me. It means that on any given Sunday morning I am safely held and thoroughly equipped by these special, life-giving words.

A number of years ago I asked another vicar how he coped conducting funeral services that were at times so full of grief and pain. His advice to me was 'to lean into the liturgy - to let the liturgy take the strain.' I have never forgotten that and have found it to be good advice for vicar and congregation alike. In your grief, you do not have to find the right words - appropriate and meaningful words are right there for you.

For one good reason or another, sometimes upon arriving at church, we are not quite ready or eager to worship God straight away.[92] That need not matter. The liturgy gives us the words when we have none of our own - honouring, uplifting, glory-giving words.[93]

Paul Zahl calls liturgical worship 'Bible-based verticality'.[94] The formal Bible reading part of the service is not the only time you are going to hear the Bible in the service. Good liturgy is full of the Bible which means it is good for your soul. Reading the Bible is always a good thing; hearing it read is often better; hearing it and having the opportunity to speak it out yourself, is best of all - ask any teacher.[95]

Worship is also 'vertical' in that it looks up before it looks out. It does build the congregation up and do us good, but first and foremost it is directed towards God. It is our

---

[92] Grief, pain, anxiety, sadness can all rob us of our joy in God.

[93] By the way - come as you are! Pretence is the enemy of true intimacy with God. If you are not feeling it, allow the words you hear and read to wash over you and the Holy Spirit will meet you right where you are.

[94] Paul Zahl in , *Exploring the Worship Spectrum*, 23

[95] Actor and Christian David Suchet has painstakingly recorded the whole of the Bible, which I listen to everyday. It is available as a CD set or digital download.

expression of love, devotion and commitment towards our loving God.

Beware

However, liturgy should have a spiritual health warning attached to it. I would even go as far as to say that it is *dangerous*. Allow me to explain using a classic book dating back to 1678.

John Bunyan's *Pilgrim's Progress* is a book that tells the story of Christian, making his way along life's journey from his hometown, the 'City of Destruction' to the 'Celestial City', heaven. Along the way he meets several characters who light up his journey and help make him who he is. One such character is Mr Formalist. He and his close companion, Mr Hypocrisy come from the land of Vainglory. The outward appearance of Mr Formalist would suggest he too is a Christian. He knows all the right words - he looks and sounds like the real thing. But whilst he knows all the outward forms of religion, little or nothing of the inward reality of faith is his. The gospel is certainly in his head but it hasn't penetrated his heart.

I have met people who can recite liturgy off by heart, but they have not embraced the truth of the words for themselves. It remains theoretical rather than personal. Being able to recite the Creed or the Lord's Prayer or any of the liturgy used in church on a Sunday, will not save you. Only knowing and trusting in the Saviour, Jesus Christ can do that.

Words are Important

Corporate worship lies at the heart of the Christian life. We use the words we say and sing to give expression to what we believe, which in turn shapes who we are. They give us our identity. Therefore it is important that the words we use in our worship services are grounded in truth. Right thinking about God, ourselves and the world around us is essential in the forming and creating of liturgy.

Every one of us arrives at church with a whole host of emotions whirling around within us. The events of the past week, stresses and strains of ordinary everyday life and national or international stories all form a cocktail of highs and lows. We do not come to church to forget these things but rather to bring them into the light and in some cases have our perspective on them adjusted by God's grace and truth. Good liturgy helps us to, as it were 'join the dots' between everyday life and spiritual truth.

They both form and inform each other. Too often we create a divide between the sacred and the secular, believing some things to be spiritual and others not. But the truth is that everything is spiritual! God is interested and invested in every part of our lives. As complex human beings we need not leave any part of who we are at the church door with the intention of picking it up again on the way out.

Disciple-Making

The Bible calls the people who Jesus called to follow him around and learn to do what he did, 'disciples'. Where he went, they followed and in the process, over the three years of his earthly ministry, they gradually became more and more like him in their beliefs and actions.

As Christians we are modern-day disciples - learning to be like Jesus. One way that this happens is through the time we spend together in church - notably through the words we share one with another. The liturgy we use forms us, teaches us, re-orients us and if we allow it to go down deep, it makes us more like Jesus.

Disciples are undoubtedly formed in many ways: in families, through personal times of prayer and reading the Bible, through significant friendships and indeed through everyday life experiences. The difficult ones tend to be especially of use in the disciple-making process! But what we do together and who we become as 'Church' is hugely significant. My own testimony as a church-goer for fifty-plus years is that it would be impossible for me to over-estimate the importance of what I have heard, said and participated in, at church.

Stanley Hauerwas says that a church must be 'a community of character.'[96] By this he does not mean we should be made up of interesting and colourful people (although we often are!) or that we should be genuinely likeable people (although we should!). He argues we should be a community learning to worship God in spirit and in truth.[97] He raises the importance of the gathered Christian community and in so doing reminds me that every single part of our worship service is important.

No church service, regardless of its tradition is perfect. My prayer is that if you decide to pay your local church a visit, you will find the words you hear and are asked to

---

[96] Stanley Hauerwas, *A Community of Character: Towards a Constructive Christian Social Ethic.*

[97] John 4. 24

join in with, to be life-giving, enlivening and powerful. May the words and those that deliver them do you good.

Thirteen
Why Bother with Church?

❊ ❊ ❊

> He who does not have the church as his mother,
> does not have God as his father.
> *Augustine of Hippo*

I have heard it so many times - why do I need to bother with church? Can't I just love God, follow Him and try to honour him without going to church? Technically yes - realistically no. Allow me explain.

Being a Christian is not about obtaining a ticket to heaven when you die. I know that's not always what Christians or churches have told you but historically we have done you a disservice in leading you to believe this. Being a Christ follower (that is what a Christian is) is about having true life in *this* world *and* the next. How? By knowing the author of life, the source of true life, the one through whom life (and death) make sense. OK, so how can we possibly know him?

The Bible tells us that when Jesus walked the earth, he was God in flesh and bones; that he lived, died, rose again and is present with us now by means of the Holy Spirit. We encounter God today because He lives in us by His Spirit, and He is therefore present and active today primarily through lives that are surrendered to Him. This is why when we meet together in church, we can claim "God is here!"

So when you have a joyous conversation with a fellow believer at church, you can also have an encounter with God. When you are led in song by a fellow believer - you encounter God. When you are led in prayer at church, you encounter God.

And here's the paradox: you can also encounter God in all the difficulties and frustrations and maddening things about church because in and through them, God in His grace teaches you, corrects you and helps you to grow. I am afraid it is true - the very people that may make you want to skip church or give up on it altogether, are often the very people God uses to mould, re-make and heal you. Under God's great plan, they help you become the best version of you.

It stands to reason that it is so much more difficult to be changed or renewed sitting on your couch at home[98]. God's chosen or preferred means of working out His transformative purposes in our lives is in and through the godly people He brings alongside us - the group we call church.

At various points in this book I have made it quite clear that the Church is far from perfect - after all we are just a group of imperfect people. In my experience, God loves to use the imperfections in others to iron out some of my failings. In church, we bump up against each other, we sometimes fall out or disagree with each other, we both cause offence and take offence easily. But in so doing, God by His Holy Spirit is at work amongst us. We truly discover what lies deep within; we recognise our need for forgiveness and for a Saviour and we throw ourselves upon his love and mercy. In short, we learn what it is to be truly human and to follow Christ - to be a Christian. Some would say it is moving from the theory of faith to the reality.

---

[98] I am not saying impossible.

There is a word I have used more than once in this chapter that I want to elaborate on - that word is *encounter*. Every time we walk into church there is a chance to encounter the Living God. He is ready and willing to meet with us - often the only thing stopping or limiting this is my lack of expectation. If I expect nothing I will most likely get nothing. If I am cynical or dubious, I am unlikely to experience or encounter the presence of God. Conversely, if I am hungry, expectant and open to that encounter, then God is always ready and willing to meet with us.

This was entirely my experience on 28th June 1984. My childhood hadn't been the easiest to negotiate. Despite growing up in a loving and stable home, in my early teens I began to experience significant anxiety issues. Today this would be nothing new but back then poor mental health was not so common (or at least not so publicly acknowledged). For a couple of years, I was afraid to go to church although I never stopped believing in God.

Through the faithful prayers and support of friends and family I began to attend services again and began to enjoy the experience. But on the evening of 28th June

1984, I had an encounter with God. The speaker that evening was Jim Cockburn, a local Secondary School teacher and the essence of what he said, I had probably heard many times before. But on that particular night, it was as if God was speaking personally to me. Almost as if he was using my name. I knew I needed to make a response and shortly after I prayed a heartfelt prayer that was to change my life forever.

Could God have spoken to me on my own at home? I suppose so - he is God after all! But my experience is that a gathering of believing, praying, worshipping people is most often His chosen place to meet us and speak to us.

For me, if there is one word that sums up church it would have to be *encounter*. I can't prescribe how you will encounter God at church but I know that He is ready, willing and able to meet with you - especially if your heart is open to that possibility. I have already told you how an encounter with God in church changed my life forever way back in 1984. Here are four other encounters that I want to share with you because all four are so completely different from each other:

A few years ago I led a congregation called Café Church for about three years. This very informal service attracted all sorts of people including many who were homeless, those with mental health issues, ex-offenders and some who were simply disillusioned with more traditional forms of church. I remember sitting in my first Café Church service feeling a genuine mix of terror and exhilaration! But every week the honesty and authenticity of those attending led to genuine encounters with God. There was no room for masks or pretence at this form of church. I learnt how to preach whilst being heckled, how to pray for the lost, the lonely and those who society thought of as the lowest, and how to go home to my nice warm house knowing some fellow worshippers would be in the park or in shop doorways.[99]

As we worshipped as a community we undoubtedly encountered God in ways and with people that doesn't happen very often.

I had a very different sort of encounter with God when actively inviting the Holy Spirit to touch, fill and heal me. Christians worshipping in what is loosely called the

---

[99] I don't say this flippantly. It is the reality of working with extremely needy people. Some you can't help - some don't want to be helped.

Charismatic wing of the Church believe that God (by his Spirit) is more imminently present in a worship service and that He wants our encounter with Him to be undeniable and in some cases physical. On one such occasion I found myself being literally swept off my feet and lying on the ground in a wonderful state of peace and tranquility. ….

Before, during and after a powerful experience of God such as this it is worth remembering that we seek the Giver not the gift - the One who brings the experience not the experience itself. There is a great danger in becoming what might be termed 'spiritual experience junkies'.

Now come with me to a completely different kind of church and a very different setting. As I have already explained, in some churches the Gospel reading (containing the words of Jesus) is read from within the main body of assembled people. A procession takes place with the book containing the Gospel reading lifted high and everyone turns to face the place from where it is read. A few years ago I found myself in a service supporting a friend who was taking the next step of commitment in his faith journey. The church was packed and as the Bishop read the Gospel reading from the heart/middle of the church, I struggled to see him at all. All I could see was incense rising from the spot where he was reading. As the incense rose coupled with the Bishop's powerful reading from the Bible, I had a new and hugely impactful experience of the presence of God. The incense seemed to add new weight to the words we heard - almost as if it carried the words (and something of their meaning) and enabled them to hover over us as we breathed them in. It was a weighty, significant moment. Up until then (and indeed since), incense had not played any meaningful role in my worship experience but on this occasion, God took me by surprise and reminded again of the importance of his words in the Bible.

I have shared with you three very different encounters with God that I have had in church - the fourth is different again. St Paul's Cathedral in London is a hugely impressive structure. Architecturally it is a marvel with its huge dome in the centre and its rich history covering the Great Fire of London in 1666, through two World Wars and beyond. When you enter from the west end of the building, it cannot fail to take your breath away leaving you with a sense of the awesomeness of Almighty God.

I have experienced God on several occasions worshipping in the cathedral. The resonance of the great organ takes me to another place; the beautiful harmonies of the choir give me a glimpse of the worship going on in heaven; being seated and completely still can also bring the reality of God's presence home to me. What those serving at the cathedral *do* is important (and how well they do it) but of greater significance is my openness of heart and expectation of an encounter with the Living God.

Why have I told you about these four very different encounters with God in various churches? Two main reasons:

- No-one can prescribe how you or I will encounter God in church. Any attempt to do so equates to manipulation and ought to lead to questions as to whether it is God being encountered at all. All that is needed is an open heart - what the Bible refers to as being hungry or thirsty for God.[100]
- God can be encountered in all forms of church across every tradition and denomination. Your hunger and

---

[100] Matthew 5. 6, John 6. 33-35.

thirst can be met in all sorts of different ways at a range of different places.

I have attempted to lift the lid on church in this book. By offering you insight and understanding about what goes on, my hope is that the church will be more accessible to you and that these various practices could be special and meaningful to you as you seek God for yourself.

You are now ready to give church a try. If someone gave you this book, then chat through your first experience with them - they may even go with you and metaphorically 'hold your hand'. As I have already said, you may need to be persistent and go a few times before you can make up your mind whether church is for you. You may also need to try a few different churches to see where you best fit.

What I do know is that although church is broken and fallible, the God whom we seek and worship is not. He is for you - He loves you - He is near - and relationship with Him is possible for everyone. As you seek Him, may you find riches beyond compare are yours - life in abundance for this world and the next.

Also available by Andy Johnson

The Journey: A Simple Rule of Life
ISBN 9781719527781

Am I more of a disciple than a year ago?
Am I am better disciple?
How would I even know?

The trouble with Christian discipleship is that it can be somewhat of a nebulous concept. Not knowing whether you can even measure these things, you have to trust the process: do certain things, engage in tried and trusted practices and then you can have greater confidence about what the end result will look like.

A Rule of Life can help you live with intention and purpose in the present moment. It enables you to clarify your most important values and can help you live by them.

> "Thoroughly recommended"
> The Rt Revd Pete Broadbent
> Former Bishop of Willesden

Printed in Great Britain
by Amazon